The Russian Campaign
of 1812

To
Gladys Elloran Phillips
and
Robert C. Leitz

The Russian Campaign of 1812

The Memoirs of a Russian Artilleryman

Translated and Edited by
Alexander Mikaberidze and Peter G A Phillips

Pen & Sword
MILITARY
AN IMPRINT OF PEN & SWORD BOOKS LTD.
YORKSHIRE - PHILADELPHIA

First published in Great Britain in 2023 by
PEN AND SWORD MILITARY
An imprint of
Pen & Sword Books Limited
Yorkshire – Philadelphia

Copyright © Alexander Mikaberidze and Peter G A Phillips, 2023

ISBN 978 1 39906 794 2

The right of Alexander Mikaberidze and Peter G A Phillips to be identified as Authors of this work has been asserted by them in accordance with the Copyright, Designs and Patents Act 1988.

A CIP catalogue record for this book is available from the British Library.

All rights reserved. No part of this book may be reproduced or transmitted in any form or by any means, electronic or mechanical including photocopying, recording or by any information storage and retrieval system, without permission from the Publisher in writing.

Typeset in Times New Roman 12/16 by
SJmagic DESIGN SERVICES, India.
Printed and bound in the UK by CPI Group (UK) Ltd.

Pen & Sword Books Limited incorporates the imprints of Atlas, Archaeology, Aviation, Discovery, Family History, Fiction, History, Maritime, Military, Military Classics, Politics, Select, Transport, True Crime, Air World, Frontline Publishing, Leo Cooper, Remember When, Seaforth Publishing, The Praetorian Press, Wharncliffe Local History, Wharncliffe Transport, Wharncliffe True Crime and White Owl.

For a complete list of Pen & Sword titles please contact
PEN & SWORD BOOKS LIMITED
47 Church Street, Barnsley, South Yorkshire S70 2AS, United Kingdom
E-mail: enquiries@pen-and-sword.co.uk
Website: www.pen-and-sword.co.uk

Or

PEN AND SWORD BOOKS
1950 Lawrence Rd, Havertown, PA 19083, USA
E-mail: Uspen-and-sword@casematepublishers.com
Website: www.penandswordbooks.com

Contents

Preface		vi
Chapter I	On the Eve of War	1
Chapter II	From Vilna to the Dvina	15
Chapter III	From the Dvina to Smolensk	34
Chapter IV	From Smolensk to Borodino	57
Chapter V	From Borodino to Moscow	76
Chapter VI	From Moscow to Tarutino	93
Chapter VII	From Tarutino to Maloyaroslavets	113
Chapter VIII	From Maloyaroslavets to Vyazma	132
Chapter IX	From Vyazma to Krasnyi	149
Chapter X	From Krasnyi to Grodno	162
Index		175

Preface

Human life is short and fleeting, and many millions of individuals, who share in it, are swallowed by that monster of oblivion which is waiting for them with ever-open jaws. It is thus a very thankworthy task to try to rescue something – the memory of interesting and important events, or the leading features and personages of some epoch – from the general shipwreck of the world.

Arthur Schopenhauer,
'Art der Literatur'

Much has been written about Europe's struggle against Napoleon at the start of the nineteenth century, but many important aspects in this vast landscape of human experience remain only dimly explored. The shelves of any decent library groan under the weight of works on the British and French involvement in the Napoleonic Wars, but the travails of the Russian officers and soldiers in these conflicts attracted little attention in non-Russian languages. Moreover, due to political and ideological rivalries, linguistic difficulties and administrative hurdles, only a handful of Russian memoirs have been translated into English; consequently, Russian voices remain largely absent from the pages of historical narrative. Russian perspective, however, is essential to understanding this complex era. There is much new to learn from the vast Russian literature memoir, whose pages abound with insights and fresh perspectives. This gap has been partially filled with the publication of a handful of Russian memoirs – such

PREFACE

as those of Denis Davydov, Nadezhda Durova, Moris von Kotzebue, Boris Uxkull, Alexey Yermolov, Eduard von Löwenstern, and more recently a three-volume anthology *Russian Eyewitness Accounts* – but there remain dozens of interesting memoirs and diaries awaiting their turn in limelight.

The lengthy reminiscences of Ilya Timofeyevich Radozhitskii deserve to be ranked among the finest of the Napoleonic memoirs. Its author, the future major general, was born on 17/28 July 1788 but little is known about his childhood. Radozhitskii studied at the Imperial Orphanage (*Imperatorskii voenno-sirotskii dom*) just as Napoleon was destroying the Third and Fourth Coalitions and forging his mighty empire. In late 1806, with Russia still at war with France, the eighteen-year-old Radozhitskii enlisted as a sub-lieutenant in the Khersonskii Artillery Garrison where he served for two years. In the fall of 1808, he transferred to the 2nd Field Artillery Brigade, where, through much persistence and meritorious service, he rose to the rank of a lieutenant in January 1810. Two years later he found himself in the 3rd Light Company of the 11th Artillery Brigade of the 6th Infantry Corps.

Napoleon's invasion of Russia marked a turning point in his life. Radozhitskii was involved in the fighting from the first days of the war. He distinguished himself during the fighting at Ostrovno (July 25) where he was wounded and decorated with the Order of St. Anna (4th class) for gallantry. He then witnessed the battles of Smolensk (August 16-18), Lubino (Valutina Gora, August 19) and Borodino (September 7); he lamented the surrender of Moscow on September 14 and celebrated the Russian victories at Vyazma and Krasnyi two months later. From November to December 1812, he was an eyewitness to the catastrophe that engulfed the Grande Armée, which he vividly describes in his memoirs.

In 1813-1814, Radozhitskii took part in the War of the Sixth Coalition, serving with distinction at Bautzen (May 20-21), Katzbach (August 26, awarded the Order of St. Vladimir 4th class with ribbon for gallantry), Leipzig (October 16-19, received the Order of St. Vladimir 3rd class for military prowess) and Paris (March 30-31, 1814), where he celebrated the end of the war. Promoted to staff captain in January 1815, he barely had time to rest from the long return march from France when he was assigned to the Russian Expeditionary Corps that was dispatched to fight Napoleon upon his escape from Elba. Yet, the Russian corps arrived too late to contribute to Napoleon's final defeat and Radozhitskii saw no combat. Instead, he took pleasure in the French and German landscapes and indulged in theater and arts.

After the end of the war, Radozhitskii remained in the military and enjoyed a successful career. He was first assigned to His Imperial Majesty's Suite on Quartermaster Service (the precursor to the Russian General Staff) and was promoted to captain in 1817. Two years later he was already a lieutenant colonel. After a brief retirement, he returned to active service in 1823 and was given command of the 1st Battery Company of the 22nd Artillery Brigade. In 1824-1828 he commanded the 4th Battery Company of the 21st Artillery Brigade and the Caucasian Mobile Reserve Park. In 1828, he was deployed in the Caucasus and took part in the Russo-Ottoman War; during the fighting at Erzerum, he was introduced to the great Russian poet Alexander Pushkin, with whom he struck friendship. After the war, Radozhitskii served in the Artillery Department of the Ministry of War but did not stay there for long as he was soon chosen to direct the main Russian armament factory at Tula. Promoted to colonel in December 1835, he was recognized with the Order of St. George (4th class) for twenty-five years of unblemished service in the officer ranks. After a second retirement in 1838-1839, he once again returned to active duty and commanded artillery garrisons in Georgia, taking part in the battles against the Caucasian mountaineers during the Caucasian War in the 1840s. His performance was noticed and recognized with the promotion to the rank of major general in 1850, when he retired for the final time. He spent the remaining eleven years of his life in the

PREFACE

city of Voronezh, where he passed away in April 1861 and was buried at the local Pokrovskii Monastery.

Aside from his military career, Radozhitskii also enjoyed literary success. He corresponded with many leading literary figures and published his articles in prominent contemporary newspapers and journals such as *Severnaya pchela, Otechestvennye zapiski*, etc. He was a prolific author, producing four-volume memoir on the Napoleonic Wars, a multi-volume reminiscence on his experiences during the Russo-Ottoman War and the Caucasian War, as well as numerous ethnographic essays that provide fascinating insights into the lives of the North Caucasian mountaineers. An active member of the Moscow Society of Gardeners, Radozhitskii spent years collecting and studying plants, introducing new species, and building one of the largest private botanical libraries in Russia. He poured his heart and soul into an illustrated fifteen-volume encyclopedia of world flora that he spent most of his life writing but was never published.

Radozhitskii wrote four volumes of reminiscences on the Napoleonic Wars, dedicating each volume to the specific campaign: volume one traces his experiences during Napoleon's invasion of Russia, or the Patriotic War as this conflict is known in Russia, while subsequent volumes examine the campaigns of 1813, 1814 and 1815 respectively. Radozhitskii kept notes while campaigning and rewrote them into memoirs shortly after the war ended; excerpts from his writings began to appear in the Russian literary journals and newspapers already in the early 1820s. Written with flair and an eye for a memorable scene or detail, these reminiscences rivaled historical novels of the period, painting a grand, almost Biblical, panorama of Russia's struggle against Napoleon with a lowly artillery officer caught in the middle of it all and quickly maturing from a novice to a veteran, inured to the horrors of war but still retaining his humanity. Radozhitskii's memoirs captivated readers for decades - Leo Tolstoy himself could not resist them, consulting them extensively while writing his epic *War and Peace* and incorporating more than one scene into the novel. Such appropriations underscore just what a wonderful work of literature Radozhitskii has produced.

Alexander Mikaberidze
Shreveport Louisiana
March 31, 2022

Chapter I

On the Eve of War

Napoleon, from the height of his bellicose monarchy, had sown terror across Europe. His name terrorized the German rabble [*chern'*], as well as the Russian one, who thought of him only as the Antichrist because of the similarity between his name and the apocalyptic Apollyon. He turned into a bone of contention for Russian sages. In officers' conversations about Napoleon, we often regretted that Providence had not arranged for him to encounter Suvorov - the scythe had not hit a rock.[1] Maybe the Russian Hannibal would have prevented the great Corsican from ascending the throne of the Bourbon dynasty. But the laws of Providence are immutable: after his Egyptian campaign Napoleon used his bayonets to proclaim himself as the head of the Republic. His subsequent exploits eclipsed his earlier accomplishments and firmly secured his authority and, as the new century dawned, Europe witnessed the rise of the new Emperor of the French.

Plenty has been written about Napoleon. Most writers disparage him without mercy, barking like [fabulist Ivan] Krylov's lapdog at the elephant;[2] in the meantime, generals, ministers, and legislators copy his methods of war, policy, and even governance. He was an

---

1 Radozhitskii uses a well-known Russian proverb "nashla kosa na kamen" which is similar to the English "you have met your match."

2 Radozhitskii refers to famous Russian fabulist Ivan Krylov's story *An Elephant and a Lapdog*, which is about a little lapdog (Mos'ka) that saw an elephant being led through the town for a show and began barking furiously at it. Her neighbor dog asked, "Mos'ka, why are you barking? Don't you see the elephant is not paying any attention to you. He does not even know you exist!" But the lapdog responded, "I know. But other dogs may hear me and think, 'This Mos'ka is tough! Look at her, she is barking at an elephant himself!"

THE RUSSIAN CAMPAIGN OF 1812

enemy to all nations of Europe whom he sought to subjugate to his autocracy. He was also a genius when it came to war and politics, so people admired and imitated the genius in him while despising him as their enemy.

The glory of his exploits made people forget about the lowly beginnings of the Corsican. Waiting for his final blow, terrified Europe gazed in awe and fear at the great Emperor of the French. After crushing Germany's last effort to free itself from him [in 1809],[3] it seemed that Napoleon could simply wipe some powers off the map of Europe; but the conqueror instead chose to enhance his pedigree by marrying into the ancient dynasty of the Emperors of Germany.[4] To capture the mighty king's daughter has always been the heroes' ambition in novels and tales. And Napoleon had accomplished this, adding a new [romantic] page to his own remarkable novel, placing his newborn on the throne of the Roman Caesars and bequeathing him the dream of owning the world. Yet there was another power [Britain] still breathing and fighting but perhaps the reason the terrible conqueror has spared its existence was because of the powerful Russia he had to contend with. Napoleon admired his great rival [Russia] but he was also nourishing a hydra close to her heart, resurrecting a political phoenix [Duchy of Warsaw] from the ashes of the destroyed Sarmatia.[5] Only Russia and England remained undaunted by this giant: the former because of her strength on land, the latter due to her dominance of the seas. They both sharpened their swords to overcome his greatness.

I will no longer dwell on this extraordinary man who laid the foundation for political transformations of future generations; neither will I discuss the breakdown of the alliance between the mighty

---

[3] The War of the Fifth Coalition that pitted Austria against France and Russia in 1809.

[4] In 1810, Napoleon married Austrian Archduchess Marie Louise, the eldest daughter of Francis II, Holy Roman Emperor and Emperor of Austria.

[5] Radozhitskii refers to Napoleon's establishment of the Duchy of Warsaw in 1808. Sarmatia was legendary and the unofficial name of the Polish-Lithuanian Commonwealth, popularized in the 17th century.

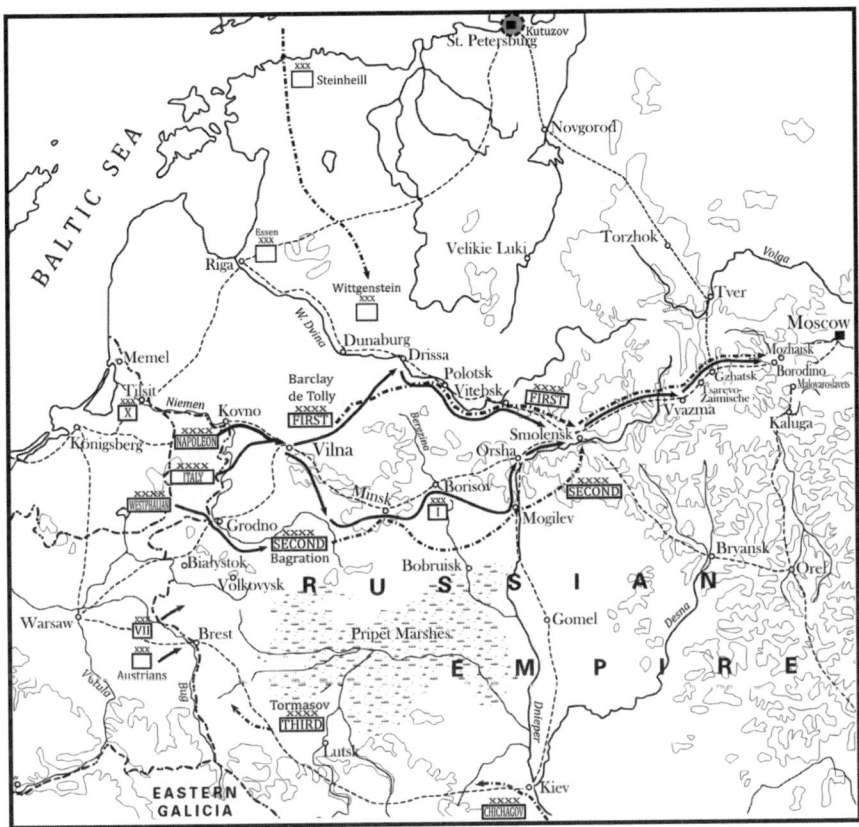

Napoleon's invasion and the Russian Retreat.

sovereigns [Napoleon and Alexander], their preparations for war or the size of their armies and so forth. All of this is well known and has no place in my work. Instead, let me regale you with my own exploits.

On the eve of the war in 1812, the 3rd Light Company of the 11th Artillery Brigade,[6] where I served as a lieutenant, was at its canton-quarters in the town of Nesvizh in the Minsk province. Our brigade belonged to the 6th Corps of Lieutenant General Essen II.[7]

---

6 The 11th Artillery Brigade also included the 4th Light Company and the 2nd Battery (Heavy) Company, for a total of thirty-six cannon.

7 Magnus Gustav von Essen (1758-1813) commanded a corps of observation which was later reorganized into the 6th Corps. In early June 1812, Essen was appointed the military governor of Riga and then governor general of Lifland, Estland, and Courland, where he mobilized and commanded forces during the war.

THE RUSSIAN CAMPAIGN OF 1812

In Nesvizh we lived splendidly, not thinking about the French; few of our officers preoccupied themselves with politics. We occasionally learned political news from local newspapers but quickly forgot all about them in the clatter of our carefree daily life. Only one man, N... (one of our non-commissioned officers), an intelligent man who read both the Scripture and the Moscow newspapers, was horrified by Napoleon. Tormented by the ghosts of his imagination, he preached to us that the Antichrist himself, Apollyon or Napoleon, was gathering great evil forces near Warsaw for no other purpose but to destroy our Mother Russia; that with the help of Beelzebub, who invisibly supported him, he would inevitably capture Moscow and conquer the entire Russian nation, and soon thereafter the world would face the Day of Judgment. We laughed at such absurdities, which greatly annoyed N. who kept calling us godless. And he was not joking about it, for he was deeply convinced in his own prophecies. Constantly imbibing tobacco, he did his best to persuade us and kept referring to the ninth chapter of the Revelation which, he said, described Napoleon as the leader of the dreaded army with lions' teeth, breastplates of iron, and scorpions' tails.[8] He became so emotionally shaken by all of this that when he was sent on a mission to Moscow, he told everyone who would listen that Napoleon was the Antichrist. So afterwards we were quite surprised when the French did invade Russia and occupied Moscow. Captured during the campaign, N. was released from his imprisonment after the French seized Moscow and appeared at our camp at Krasnaya Pakhra.[9] The suffering had altered his features:

---

8 Revelation, 9:6-11: "During those days men will seek death, but will not find it; they will long to die, but death will elude them. The locusts looked like horses prepared for battle. On their heads they wore something like crowns of gold, and their faces resembled human faces. Their hair was like women's hair, and their teeth were like lions' teeth. They had breastplates like breastplates of iron, and the sound of their wings was like the thundering of many horses and chariots rushing into battle. They had tails and stings like scorpions, and in their tails they had power to torment people for five months. They had as king over them the angel of the Abyss, whose name in Hebrew is Abaddon, and in Greek, Apollyon."

9 Krasnaya Pakhra was a village on the Kaluga road, southwest of Moscow.

his pale sunken face, clouded eyes, and obsessive consumption of tobacco all pointed to a man who had completely lost his mind. As he bid farewell to us, he warned us that the Doomsday was approaching. But maybe N. was not the only one who had lost his mind since all readers of the Revelation shared his fate: some dreamed up visions, others imagined the Antichrist in reality. Such phenomena are rare but nothing special: they are caused by powerful angst inside the brain. People, who are engaged in modern political developments, could easily foresee the future by comparing the past with the present since similar causes produce similar consequences.

France under Napoleon was stronger than Russia; his vast army stood at our very frontiers. Most people were convinced of the invincibility of Napoleon... What kind of a Russian would not have been terrified to see this invincible colossus, ready to invade his beloved Motherland? Whose heart would not have shuddered at the very thought of foreign subjugation? Such emotional anguish could certainly produce visions and imaginary revelations, which were then partially confirmed by subsequent events. So, perceptive political observers could indeed foresee the future several years ahead by observing current affairs, discerningly looking to the past while pondering the future.

Shortly after N. made his prophecy, local authorities in Nesvizh arrested spies who had disguised themselves as comedians or magicians. Apparently, Napoleon's methods of war included dispatching, on the eve of war, legions of spies and instigators into the hostile country so they could facilitate the advance of his victorious army. The majority of these spies appeared under the guise of land surveyors or Polish *komorniks* who, simultaneously to our officers of the Quartermaster Service, conducted surveys of the vicinity of Nesvizh. I especially noticed their activity on one occasion. I was assigned new quarters in town and as soon I stepped over the threshold of my new home, I came across a *komornik* surrounded by mathematical tools and plans. I told him to clear out of the house which was given to me by the decision of the Jewish *kahal*[10] and presented to him a Jewish foreman who confirmed my words. The *komornik* answered in Polish, but in an awkward dialect, that he had been quartered here with the permission of Prince R[adziwill] and would not tolerate being banished from this place by anyone. As the conversation between us heated up, the frightened Jewish foreman fled while the Polish *komornik* suddenly revealed himself as a Frenchman... Immediately guessing who he was, I rushed to my commander, but while we searched for the *gorodnichii*,[11] the *komornik* disappeared without leaving even a piece of paper behind him.

Meanwhile, as spies infiltrated the border areas of European Russia and set fire to the best buildings in various cities, the governments of the Allied Powers were extraordinarily preoccupied in diplomatic subtleties as they both sought to protect the political rights of their sovereigns. While these events were unfolding, the two powerful but rival sovereigns moved their armies closer to the borders of their realms.

In our private pursuits officers from my brigade restricted themselves to the area surrounding Nesvizh and the first two months of the year [1812] were spent in amusements. In addition to ordinary dance gatherings on Sundays, which are called *redoubts* in Poland and are attended by cute *panienkas* [young ladies] with fresh [female] delights, our commanders also arranged evening balls. We celebrated New Year's Eve with parties, and then danced our way through the *maslyanitsa*[12], indulging ourselves with sweet sentimentality under a pleasant haze of intoxication. Older officers were frightened of Napoleon, seeing in him a terrible conqueror, the new Attila, while

---

10 A Jewish community council.

11 In the 19th century Russian, *gorodnichii* was the head of administrative- police authorities in towns.

12 *Maslyanitsa* is an ancient Russian folk holiday, originating from pre- Christian times, that is celebrated during the last week before Great Lent. While similar to Mardi Gras celebrations, the maslyanitsa instead features pancakes that are served with caviar, various fish, nuts, honey pies, and other garnishes and side dishes.

ON THE EVE OF WAR

we, the young, happily frolicked under Cupid's gaze, and sighed and groaned from his wounds... And then our lives were interrupted by the thunderous roar of war - we were told to prepare for a campaign. Alas! Farewell our sweet *panienkas*!

Preparations for the campaign proved not to be easy. [At last,] on 28 February [12 March] our company, together with the brigade headquarters, departed from Nesvizh. We had spent two years in these quarters, but the local residents did not come out to send us off as usually happens after a prolonged amicable billeting of troops. The reason for this apparently lay in the fact that the Poles were preoccupied with Napoleon and the desire for the rebirth of their homeland, while the Jews, who formed the majority of residents in Nesvizh, were only relieved to be rid of the dashing *Moskals*.[13] We, on the other hand, regretted leaving the place where we had lived comfortably and cheerfully and where lovely beauties had charmed us. As we departed on campaign, every one of us left with [romantic] heartache in our youthful chests. How many passionate sighs flew toward town as we marched to our first destination! How many farewell tears dampened the white handkerchiefs of beauties and ran down the whiskers of their suitors! How many secret messages of vows, pledged with kisses of fidelity, memory ribbons, locks of hair and rhymes, had been transferred from [female] handbags into [male] wallets, only to be used soon thereafter as *papillotes*[14] or to ignite a pipe. Oh youth, how charming are your endeavors!

Mounds of melting snow still covered the countryside. At the first tavern, about seven *verstas* [4.6 miles] from Nesvizh, our company commander served a farewell breakfast for a few of his friends and the *Boston*[15] companions who saw us off. The tavern presented a

---

13 *Moskal* (literally a Muscovite, that is, a person from Muscovy) is a historical term (and present-day slur) primarily used in Ukraine and Belarus referring to Russians.

14 A papillote was a piece of paper or textile that was used for curling hair.

15 Boston was a card game originating from Boston MA that became highly popular in 18th century Russia.

picture of contrast, where abundance was adjacent to scarcity and poverty side by side with wealth: in this smoky Jewish house, silver, porcelain, and clear crystals glittered with tasty food and drink, and where nothing but a watery *polugar*[16] was usually served now the delicious champagne foamed as farewell glasses were eagerly clinked and emptied at once.

From the tavern, we continued our march to Slonim, where we arrived on 4 [16] March. On the march we were not as much preoccupied with preparations for the campaign as with the memories of Nesvizh; still blissfully carefree, we sang songs and entertained, while at night we stayed in smoky and foul-smelling huts, where we purified the stifling atmosphere with tobacco smoke.

In Slonim, the wealthy landowner Marshal[17] P., in a sign of his affection for Russians, organized a ball to which our officers had been invited. Here once again we met very pretty *panienkas,* but our thoughts, remaining true to our first impressions, were preoccupied with Nesvizh. Current circumstances did not allow us to genuinely enjoy the festivities: everyone's faces were gloomy and suspicious, while the local guests seemed to have gathered, not for their enjoyment, but to appease the host. The Marshal walked self-importantly amidst numerous guests in the brightly illuminated rooms, but he seldom deigned to exchange words with anyone. It was here that we met our commander, Artillery General L.[18]

The following day, early in the morning, we received an order from General L. that upon the artillery's departure, he would inspect

---

16 *Polugar* refers to a wine (or other alcohol) that had been one quarter diluted with water.

17 Marshal was not a military title but rather referred to the title, marshal of nobility, conferred on the leaders of local nobility in given regions or towns.

18 Probably Karl Fedorovich Lowenstern who commanded the artillery in Peter Bagration's 2nd Western Army. On the eve of the war, the 11th Artillery Brigade, where Radozhitskii's company was listed, was commanded by Lieutenant Colonel A. Kotlyarov. In the spring, the brigade was assigned to the 4th Infantry Corps, whose artillery was led by Colonel I. Koilenovskii.

it on full parade. How appropriate this, we thought, straight after a ball. Unfortunately for us, a terrible storm began during the parade that morning: the sleet and wind soiled our clean uniforms and blew straight into our eyes. Dressed in parade uniforms and shivering from cold, we waited outside the city for the general, who arrived wearing just his uniform, unprotected by a greatcoat. After he departed, we changed into campaign clothing and proceeded to the town of Ruzhany. On 6 [18] March we were at Seltsy on the Yaselda River, then at Pruzhany. By 8 [20] March we reached Velikoe Selo, where we remained for a week before marching with the entire brigade through Volkovysk toward Vilna [Vilnius]. Our artillery brigade of the 6th Corps had been reassigned to the 4th Corps commanded by Adjutant General Count [Pavel] Shuvalov.

As we departed from Velikoe Selo, I was appointed campaign quartermaster of my company. My responsibilities included traveling ahead to prepare quarters, to find river crossings suitable for artillery and to procure forage for our horses. This last was a particularly difficult task because there were no supply depots established along our route. Maybe the government, out of extra precaution, chose not to spend money on a region where it was preparing to engage the enemy. Be that as it may, every night we had to issue receipts for any forage that we procured.

As we travelled from Volkovysk, I [successfully] organized ferries so our artillery could cross the Zelva and Nieman Rivers at Pyaski and Masty. But procuring sufficient forage proved to be very challenging. The Polish gentry never voluntarily provided hay in exchange for receipts, written in a language alien to them (the majority of Russian Poles cannot read Russian) and so we were compelled to resort to force to obtain anything we could. Thus, at the manor belonging to Count S., offer receipts though I did, I was denied any hay. So, I went to inspect the yard and, noticing some hay in the loft of the stables, I called upon my troops to have it removed. Upon seeing from the window of his magnificent house that a dozen soldiers were preparing, in his view, to plunder his estate, the count came out and assailed me with threats that he would immediately travel to his friend, General B. and complain about the outrageous act that I was about to commit. He threatened that if I did not depart at once, he would gather his servants and throw me out. The count was choking with anger as he probably had never encountered a more discourteous man than me. Calmly and respectfully, I answered His Excellency that I was not afraid of his threats because I was carrying out the will of my commanders, who allowed us to take forage by force wherever it was not given to us voluntarily, and there was no other means of feeding the horses, horses that were, of course, the property of the state. I again asked him to give the needed amount of hay under a receipt. Otherwise, I told him, I would be compelled to take it by force, and that, if I encountered any resistance from his servants, I would have to bring up cannon and treat them as rebels challenging the authority of our government. Meanwhile, I added, he could complain about my actions to anyone he chose. Facing such an unyielding artilleryman, the Count left at once, and, fuming with rage, ordered forage to be given to my men, while he dressed up and went to complain about me to his friend General B. My company was then commanded by senior Lieutenant G. on whose orders I so boldly acted everywhere, so, it was he who was reprimanded by our superiors for discomforting the troubled count. We had no further problems with foraging since, following strict discipline on the march, we paid for everything we consumed: not a single chicken perished without us paying for it.

The closer we got to Vilna, the more we suffered from a lack of forage and, for me, the challenge of finding it only increased. Residents had used their supplies to feed their own cattle during the winter and the fresh grass had not yet appeared, even though the snow had melted in the fields. Therefore, the locals guarded what little remained of their hay or straw like their precious jewels. At the

ON THE EVE OF WAR

village of Benyakony, near Lida, one old and ailing *pan Chorąży*[19] even dared to refuse me any fodder. And since he was not a count, I acted more decisively with him. The poor chap immediately ordered an omelet and a bottle of wine to be served and began to treat me, while he, groaning from gout, kept saying, "Oh my! Misfortune begets misfortune!" Preoccupied with my business, I did not heed his words, but he carefully chose them. Maybe he was secretly instructed to keep reserve supplies of everything for foreign visitors, and [was upset that] he now had to give some to the Moskals [Russians]! Besides, with gout twisting your feet, you will inevitably start intoning, "Misfortune begets misfortune!"

In early April we arrived at our quarters near the city of Vilna. Two artillery companies from our [11th Artillery] Brigade were deployed at Bolshie and Malye Soleshniki, while the 3rd Light Company, in which I served, was deployed at the village of Yashuny,[20] some 25 *verstas* [16.5 miles] from the city. On 10 [22] April, our Emperor deigned to pass through Lida on his way to Vilna and inspected our troops *en route*. At Bolshie Soleshniki, our brigade commander, [Lieutenant] Colonel Kotlyarov, introduced some orderlies to His Majesty, who praised them and granted them monetary awards.

Throughout April, just as [Russian and French] diplomats were engaged in final negotiations and Napoleon concentrated his forces on our borders, we remained at our quarters.

In May, the order of the Commander in Chief[21] revealed to us that current circumstances pointed toward war against the French being imminent. Three artillery companies of the 11th Brigade gathered at Bolshie Soleshniki for inspection conducted by the head of the army's

---

19 Chorąży or khorunzhyi in Russia was originally a military rank in Poland that designated a warrior bearing a standard. This function later evolved into a noble title granted to leaders of local militias.

20 Jašiūnai, in modern-day Lithuania.

21 Mikhail Barclay de Tolly, commander of the 1st Western Army and the Minister of War.

artillery, Count [Alexander] Kutaisov. Just a few days later we were again inspected by our corps commander, Count [Pavel] Shuvalov. Such inspections continued throughout the army. At that time, I was sent on a mission to Bobruisk and Slonim, where I was supposed to bring back artillerymen recovering at local hospitals. So, I happened to pass through Nesvizh and memories of past delights awakened in my heart. I could not deny myself the pleasure of walking in solitude in the deserted Alba, the beautiful menagerie of Prince Radziwill's estate outside the city.[22] As I entered this charming grove, my imagination evoked images of the past – it was here, under the shade of birch trees that we gathered to enjoy nature, lay on fresh grass and breathed fragrant flowers; it was there, under lime trees, that we listened to nightingales and echoed their gentle sounds with our passionate sighs; it was there, under the arching branches of oak trees and under cool evening breath, that we enjoyed robust tea and, while water boiled in the samovar, entertained ourselves with various games. Here a rosy brunette had given a ribbon to her admirer, while over there a shy blonde had sweetly smiled at one of her own, which made him sigh and dream of her every day. The ladies occasionally dared to sail with us in boats on the lake, following us into a thicket of reeds, where we chased the proud swans... As a wise man once said, we live in our memories! And so the memories of the past delights in the deserted Alba brought several minutes of joy to my cheerless reality.

In Nesvizh, life had taken a strange turn: obviously disconcerted, people appeared with faces that were downcast and pitiful. Led by Dominican monks, large groups of school children and students were marching around the town, carrying colourful scarves on poles by way of banners, beating drums and shouting militant cries. I was amazed to see them, so I approached their half-shaved leader, and asked the meaning behind it all. "Drilling," he answered. "What

---

22 Polish noblemen and composer Prince Maciej Radziwiłł (1749 – 1800) maintained a resplendent estate in Alba, near Nesvizh (Nieśwież), where he cultivated gardens and kept a company of actors, musicians and dancers.

ON THE EVE OF WAR

for?" I inquired. "To set an example," he countered. This answer seemed suspicious to me, so I looked for the *gorodnichii* and told him that such disciplining seemed inappropriate for students in present circumstances. "Do not worry, they are just being mischievous!" responded the *gorodnichii*, knowing well what this mischief aimed at: he belonged to the more truthful Poles.

I found nothing remarkable in Minsk except for dull seclusion. I then reached Bobruisk, where I spent three days carrying out my mission. I witnessed the vigorous work of our engineers who were busy constructing the recently founded fortress. They kept repairing the main parapet, which often collapsed due to the infirmness of the sandy soil. Despite our engineers' best efforts, the outer fortifications had not been completed yet.

On the way back from Bobruisk I experienced delays and difficulties in obtaining horses at every postal station. It seemed that order was gradually dismantled and everything was getting out of control. The post keepers were distracted, drivers drank and brawled, and no one wanted to look at my travel voucher. I was able to procure horses only through threats or enticements; at the Pyaski station, I had to send a formal complaint to the Lithuanian Post Office.

The 3rd Light Company, of which I was a member, long remained without a commander after [Lieutenant] Colonel Kotlyarov was given temporary command of the brigade and the 1st Company in place of Colonel Guinet, who was transferred to another brigade. By the end of May, while our company remained at the village of Yashuny, we were joined by the new commander, Lieutenant Colonel M., and Captain [Alexander] Figner, who later became a famous partisan.

In early June, our corps marched toward the border. The corps headquarters was established at Olkeniki[23] while our brigade stopped at Oishishki.[24] The corps advance guard, under the command of

---

23 Present-day Valkininkai, Lithuania.

24 Present-day Eišiškės, Lithuania.

General [Ivan] Dorokhov, was at Orany.[25] As the troops concentrated, they found themselves billeted in overcrowded quarters. The light artillery was distributed among brigades of army regiments and our company had been assigned to the 1st Brigade of the 11th Division, serving alongside the excellent Pernovskii and Kexholmskii Regiments under the command of General [Pavel] Choglokov. We then underwent several more reviews conducted by brigade and division commanders. Overall, our soldiers were well dressed and trained. They were tall and handsome, their heart burning with ardour at the idea of crossing the border to attack the French, something that had become an old habit for them.

We remained at Olkeniki for almost a week, every day waiting for the start of the campaign. Then, on 12 [24] June, we suddenly received orders to hastily return to Yashuny. The cause for such a sudden movement was the French, who had anticipated us and crossed the border over the Nieman River. At Merich, they captured all detachments from our division that had been dispatched to receive supplies from a local depot.

We covered the distance of some 40 *verstas* [26.4 miles] between Olkeniki and Yashuny in just one march. Apparently, we were not the only ones in a hurry - the war had indeed begun in earnest.

---

25 Present-day Varėna, Lithuania.

Chapter II

From Vilna to the Dvina

On 14 [26] June, the 11th Artillery Brigade marched toward Vilna and bivouacked near a tavern about three *verstas* [2 miles] from the city, in anticipation of further orders. The surrounding area had taken a wartime appearance: troops were approaching from various directions, and the roads were jammed with transports. This was a new and incredible sight for us, novice warriors, and it only increased our curiosity and excitement. It was here that our brigade commander received a dispatch with the imperial manifesto on the commencement of war against the French. The colonel, surrounded by officers, read aloud the memorable words of the imperial declaration which planted the seed of vengeance against the enemy of Russia in every Russian's heart. We were particularly inspired by the last words of the manifesto that deeply touched every one of us. "The Slavic blood, glorious for its victories, flows inside your veins. Warriors! Defend your faith, fatherland, independence. I am with you! God is against the enemy!" "To War!" shouted officers, quite content with themselves, and this warlike spark immediately touched everyone present.

If only Napoleon had known how spirited the Russians were, and how eager to fight his forces, unafraid of their numerical superiority; if only he had understood the impact of the tsar's promise that he would not lay down arms as long as a single enemy soldier remained in his realm; if only he had perceived the resolution of our emperor and the determination of the Russian people to fight him to the end: he would not then have entertained the futile hope of conquering

Russia by simply occupying her land. But *he was carried away by the inevitable doom: his destiny had to be fulfilled.*[1]

We thought that we would immediately advance toward the French, engage them on the border and drive them further back. But whoever understood political circumstances would have drawn a different conclusion: our first attack would have been rash and unsuccessful; in light of the enemy's numerical superiority, it would have been reckless to fight a battle. The French forces, which had been accustomed to victories, were at least twice as large as ours, while what can be said about their leader if not that the history of modern time has never seen anyone with so much good fortune or the ability to win? Who would have dared to face him? Who would have overcome his strategy and subtle policy? Napoleon could be defeated only with his own weapons: to adopt his political system and the manner of waging war. And so the weaker side had to turn to a military stratagem: to retreat step by step in front of a stronger enemy, lure him deeper and deeper into the woods and marshes where the lack of supplies, exhaustion from prolonged marshes and harshness of climate would have so weakened him that the weaker side could dare attacking the defenseless enemy. The destruction of Charles XII [in 1709] reawakened the memories of Russians. Napoleon, guided by his destiny, wanted to become matchless.

Until this time Russians were incapable of retreating and the very word "retreat," in their understanding, carried a rather prejudicial meaning, unbecoming to the honor of courageous warriors, who, under [Field Marshals Peter] Rumyantsev and [Alexander] Suvorov, were accustomed to always advance and win. Another commander probably would not have dared to launch a prolonged retreat and instead would have, like Leonidas,[2] 18 perished with all his warriors

---

1 Radozhitski refers to Napoleon's announcement to the Grand Armée made on the eve of war: "Russia is hurried on by fate; her destiny must be fulfilled."

2 Leonidas was a hero-king of Sparta who became famous for his leadership of the Spartans at the Battle of Thermopylae.

on the border instead of leading the enemy in his wake into the heart of the fatherland. But no matter how well prepared our campaign strategy was, it would hardly have been possible to compel the enemy, especially an enemy like Napoleon who was skilled in exploiting his opponents' mistakes, to act as we bade him. Spoiled by good fortune, he desired to rush to Moscow in one leap and finish the Russian campaign so quickly and gloriously as he did the Austrian and Prussian campaigns by capturing Vienna and Berlin. But it seems he knew Russia rather poorly and later sought to triumph over his misfortunes through the sheer force of his genius, this being something for which he was severely punished.

On 14 [26] June, the infantry corps of Generals [Nikolai] Tuchkov[3] and Count Shuvalov united and took battle positions in front of Vilna. Our 4th Corps stood on the left flank, at a place called Pogulyanki, and was adjacent to the main road that ran from Novye Troki [Trakai] to Vilna. Upon arriving we observed a vast number of troops and heard numerous stories about the French invasion. Some said that the Poles had betrayed us, joining Napoleon and that a widespread tumult could be expected among the Polish population. Such news was rather unpleasant to us but, seeing our forces brought together, we were unafraid of the enemy.

The Cossacks gathered numerous cattle from nearby villages and distributed them among the regiments for food. Everything was taking a military appearance: a strange mix of various types of troops, train, artillery, horses and cattle, a general commotion back and forward, the noise of weapons, the mooing of the oxen, neighing of horses and soldiers' banter – all of this presented a rather curious sight for those who experienced the war for their first time. The surrounding area was covered in smoke from bivouac fires. In the evening the tavern located in front of the camp caught fire. The flickering flames, seen through green brushwood illuminated by the last rays of the setting

---

3   Tuchkov commanded the 3rd Infantry Corps.

sun, only increased the beauty of this picturesque moment. Many objects attracted my gaze, and some plunged me into deep thought... As the twilight fell, our artillery was moved to the front line of the left flank.

The following day (15 [27] June) the rising sun cast its rays on the fearless Russian army deployed in battle formation in front of Vilna. With the first daylight, the music and drumbeats in every regiment announced the start of the day. Each warrior's soul was burning with desire to fight for the Fatherland. The morning cold refreshed the doughty faces of soldiers. Solemn tranquility and silence reigning in the camp seemed to conceal something ominous. As everyone awoke, bustling military life resumed: patrols were assigned their posts, guard duties determined, etc.; squads with artillery buckets rattled down to the river to fetch water; smoke kitchens soon began to smoke and the soldiers' porridge began to be prepared.

Our artillery company stood in battle formation, at the very edge of the front line of the left flank, on a hill from which we could observe the entire deployment of both corps. In front of our position there was thick brushwood that extended for a considerable distance, while behind us was the town. The morning ringing of bells announced the poignant prayers of town residents awaiting their fate. A terrible rumble could be heard in the environs. We stood ready for battle, in certain anticipation of and thinking about the enemy that was obscured from us; it seemed that he was silently making his way through the brushwood to suddenly attack us. Unexpectedly a hare jumped out of the bushes and charged toward our infantry. Everyone got alarmed, began to wave hands and run after the "deserter"; the frightened animal, with his ears pressed down, turned toward our battery. Here everyone rushed toward him with everything they found at hand, and the poor hare got under an artillerist who deliberately felled and killed him. The old bombardiers saw this hare as a good omen, saying, "It would have been a certain disaster if this hare had run across our battery. This is what happened to us at

FROM VILNA TO THE DVINA

Friedland [in 1807]." We cooked the hare, and, as we ate him for lunch, we laughed that we were probably eating some high-ranking enemy person whom a witch had turned into a hare, the symbol of cowardice.

We remained in our position all day long. Rumors claimed that the French were just 20 *verstas* [13 miles] from us at Novye Troki, where they were concentrating forces. Therefore, we were certain that a decisive battle would be fought the following day. Yet, in the evening we received the order... to retreat.

At dawn on 16 [28] June, our forces began to fall back. Our 4th Corps was the last to depart around 10 a.m. and passed through the Ostrobram suburb of Vilna. The movement itself went without any fuss and commotion, everyone proceeding in proper order, but with a clear sense of despondency. The six cannon of our company were moving at the end of the column, behind the 33rd Jagers and covered by one hundred Black Sea Leib-Cossacks.[4] As soon as we marched through the town and crossed the Willya River, we observed fires starting behind us: that was the Cossacks igniting the bridge and the city depots in order to halt the French who, moving close behind in our wake, were starting to occupy the city without a single shot.

We halted after marching for twelve *verstas* [8 miles]. Our rearguard consisted of four battalions of infantry, one hundred Cossacks and half a company of artillery, all under command of Colonel Bistrom,[5] who was ordered to cover the retreat of the third column, which was sent through the village of Varzhovka toward Kopunje. The country road led us along broken terrain and through brushwood. Halting on a field in sight of a town, the artillery occupied some local heights

---

4 The Leib-Guard Cossacks represented the elite of the Cossack forces and served in the Russian imperial guard (leib-gvardia), where they formed Life Guard Cossack Regiment and a *sotnya* of the Black Sea Cossacks.

5 Colonel Adam von Bistrom (Bistram), chef of the 33rd Jager Regiment and commander of the infantry brigade of the 11th Infantry Division of the 4th Corps. He was promoted to major general for his exploits during the battle of Maloyaroslavets.

and the skirmishers spread out in front, along the edge of the woods; everyone else took up battle positions. Staff Captain Figner moved his cannon from one hillock to another and, with a pencil in hand, drew terrain at each position; he ordered his men to load the cannon with solid shot and prepare canister as well. Not far from us, a line of transports moved from the town; Cossacks continuously delivered dispatches to Colonel Bistrom and then urged the transport drivers to move faster, eventually causing them to proceed at a trot. But we still could not hear any sound of gunfire or observe any Frenchmen. I was losing my patience out of curiosity and desire to see the terrible foe from whom everyone was retreating so hastily. We soon learned that, en route from Olkenki to Yashuny, having failed to catch up with us, our brigade's entire hospital, with all the sick, a physician, a medical orderly, and a farrier, had been captured by the French. This is a usual event for an army that retreats without a fight, for there is always something that gets lost despite all efforts to maintain order.

On 17 [29] June the troops of the third column crossed the Willya River at the village of Brizhi while we, together with the rearguard, remained across the river. I, escorting two cannon, was always the last man in the column, moving under the protection of a jager battalion. The Black Sea Cossacks were about half a *versta* behind us, and they occasionally exchanged fire with the enemy *flanquers*. The road runs mostly through broken terrain covered with brushwood.

As it was the first time that I was involved in action with artillery, I, due to my inexperience, remained concerned throughout the retreat. In anticipation of seeing the enemy my imagination frightened me with make-believe phantoms. During our rest or nightly bivouacs, the jager battalion and my two cannon deployed separately behind all other forces. The jagers set up their bivouacs, prepared porridge and rested while I remained with the skirmishers and Cossacks in constant anticipation of an enemy attack and did not dare to give orders to unharness horses or to rest myself. Oftentimes I was so exhausted by continual marching that I fell asleep leaning on a gun carriage.

FROM VILNA TO THE DVINA

My excitement and anxiety only further enflamed my imagination. Once, as I immersed into sweet dreams, I dreamt about Frenchmen rising out of brushwood and charging at me with swords in hand and, in excitement, I yelled "Fire" only to wake to see that there was no one around me except for my cannoniers who calmly lay next to the cannon. Our angry major, the battalion commander, did not allow my artillery crew to prepare porridge, so for several days they only ate biscuits.

On 18 [30] June the rearguard moved across a new bridge over the Willya River and took position on the higher opposite bank that overlooked the river. It was here that twelve battery guns, the entire 33rd Jager Regiment and two regiments of the line, Pernovskii and Kexholmskii, joined our rearguard. It seemed that we intended to wait here for the enemy who, despite our voluntary withdrawal, was still hiding in front of us. The Cossacks could be seen moving in the brushwood on the opposite side of the river and the smoke from their pistols occasionally appeared. By evening, we had gathered hay and placed tar on the wooden bridge and, surrounded by a mysterious silence, we waited for something to happen. Yet, as the night descended, the bridge was set on fire and presented a pleasant sight to us.

The following morning heavy rain began to pour and we all got wet and shivered from cold. The rearguard had barely moved some three *verstas* [2 miles] toward an abandoned settlement when it received an order to return to its initial position and wait for the enemy. But it was in vain – the enemy had hidden from us or, to be precise, directed the general advance of their main forces against the central column while we were ignored as being of no importance. We resumed our movement during the afternoon.

On 20 June [2 July], approaching Švenčionys, we observed other troops approaching the town from several directions; it signaled the concentration of the rearguards of the 3rd and 4th Corps, the main bodies of which had arrived yesterday. The main headquarters of His

Imperial Majesty was also located here. This news excited the troops and the presence of the Tsar further animated them. The regiments replenished their supplies from local magazines. Our rearguard was replaced by a new one and I had the pleasure of returning to my company after four days of apprehension and hardship. The commander-in-chief [Barclay de Tolly] reviewed us and thanked Colonel Bistrom for preserving the army's manpower by means of his sensible withdrawal.

The following day, as our entire column marched away from Švenčionys, we heard the sound of musket fire behind us. It was French cavalry encountering our men upon entering the town.

Our withdrawal from the village of Melisyan to Tverech [Tverečius] proceeded uneventfully. The troops moved on the grass that was wetted by rain. The hearty greenery of the wheat that was growing all around presented fulfilling forage for our horses. The air, refreshed by rains, revitalized our tired men. Provisions were in abundance and the canteen-keepers even satisfied our whims for some luxury products. But we frequently encountered fatigued horses lying on the road and, in swampy places, several of them lay together which delayed the progress of our artillery.

On 23 June [5 July], in the morning, we heard the sound of musket fire behind and to the left of us as it rapidly intensified. The generals began to issue orders and adjutants incessantly galloped back and forth with dispatches. But we were inside the forest where there was not enough space to deploy. The firefight quickly approached us and seemed to be waged right next to us. Surrounded by a thick forest, we could not see anything beyond the narrow road on which we were located so we kept accelerating our pace and safely came out of this engagement. It was said that the combat proved to be fierce. The enemy advance guard caught up with our rearguard, commanded by General Korff, near Daugėliškis but our men managed to cross the Disna River and destroy the bridge. The French, under protection of a thirty-gun battery, constructed a new bridge and moved across the river. Our rearguard took up positions on the nearest heights and bravely repelled the pursuers. The Wurttemberg chasseurs repeatedly launched frenzied assaults. This produced a fierce firefight quite close to the forest where our column was located. The French intensified their assault but the Russians doggedly resisted them and retreated afterwards in an orderly fashion. During a skirmish, a Cossack colonel wounded and captured the Wurttemberg Prince Hohenlohe.[6] As the fighting continued, we saw a cart pass nearby, from the woods to the main road, carrying a hussar dressed in dark-crimson [*temnomalinovyj*] uniform: his tall shako, long braids of hair hanging on either side and a thick clump of hair in the back all underscored the foreignness of this warrior to us. This was the first enemy I have ever seen so I examined him with great curiosity. His physique was that of slender man; he sat in the cart with his head bowed and eyes downcast. He had no desire to look at the Russian soldiers marching past his cart and seemed to be ashamed of his captivity – he was like a slumbering dragon.

The reason for such a fierce attack was the French desire to cut off the 3rd Corps. On our right, General Dokhturov's 6th Corps, which had got separated from the 2nd Army, was already considered lost. As we marched through the woods, we expected the French to come out charging from any direction. The Russians, unaccustomed to retreating without a fight, were unhappy that every night they had to shelter themselves inside fortified camps where the troops took up battle positions and spent the night in anticipation of an unexpected attack only to continue retreating with the first rays of daylight. The soldiers grumbled, saying, "The French must be very powerful if we have to abandon fortifications and keep running away from them." Such retrograde movements always weaken the spirit of an army.

The following day we came out of the woods onto open ground that was peppered with groves and small villages, which, however,

---

6 Prince von Hohenlohe was the colonel of the 3rd Wurttemberg Chasseurs.

were empty: the peasants had abandoned their houses to the mercy of friends and foes. Our detachments, dispatched to gather firewood and hay, oftentimes acted out of hatred toward the Poles, whom they considered as traitors, and dragged back everything they could find inside empty *folwarks*[7] and villages: one could see chairs, tables, feather-beds, blankets, curtains, tableware and crockery, various poultry and other things at our bivouacs. The commander-in-chief, in order to prevent further corruption of soldiers' morale, issued a strict order, threatening to execute anyone found in possession of appropriated items.

Count [Alexander] Osterman-Tolstoy replaced the ailing Count Shuvalov as the commander of the 4th Infantry Corps. He demanded an artillery officer for a mission, and I was immediately sent to meet him. I found the Count resting with the infantry. He lay wrapped in a felt cloak on the ground underneath a pine tree. General [Fedor von] Korff and a staff officer of the Quartermaster Service stood next to him. Upon hearing of my arrival, the Count asked me, "Do you have a horse?" "No, Your Excellency," [I replied.] "Then go and take one over there," he told me and pointed toward a hill with a few buildings. "And let an NCO escort him," he added. So I went to the *folwark* and entered the stables, where I found three good steeds and chose a black stallion for myself, telling the NCO to lead him behind me. Suddenly three beautiful young women and a young Pole appeared, like Amour and the Gratiae,[8] in front of us. Bitterly crying, they begged me to leave them their stallion on which all their hopes of escaping the French rested. It was hard not to laugh upon seeing how passionately these beauties wanted to keep the stallion. But I was implacable to their appeals and started to leave with my spoil; the wailing of the

---

7 Folwark is a Polish term for a large noble estate and agricultural enterprise that employed serfs. The term originates from the German "Vorwerk" ("farmhouse before a manor or city").

8 Gratiae or "graces" were Ancient Roman goddesses of charm, beauty, nature, human creativity and fertility.

beauties followed me, the good stallion neighed in response while the young Polish boy, with tears running down his face, ran behind me. On my return General Korff had not let me meet the Count. Upon seeing the desperate women standing with their wraps on a hill and empathizing [by their mere presence] the desperation of the Polish boy, who kept begging me to release the stallion, he told me, "My boy, give them the horse and let them be. Tell your regimental commander that the Count instructs him to give you an artillery horse and then carry out the orders you will receive." Obeying the general, I grudgingly returned that beautiful stallion which pranced behind the Polish boy to the great joy of the Polish women. I was upset that I came away empty handed, and could understand why the [Polish] beauties were unwilling to give up the horse, even though the French would take all three horses and, if they found their owners at home, treat them in accordance with the rights of the victors.

The staff officer of the Quartermaster Service showed me a map with various roads and then handed me a package and instructed me to depart. My mission was to establish communications with General Dokhturov's 6th Corps, which had been separated from the 2nd Army at the beginning of our retreat but managed to get a message through to our corps. Count Osterman wanted to verify how far away it was and where exactly it was located. I asked for an artillery horse and, armed with a sword and a *nagaika*,[9] I galloped in the ordered direction. I left the camp at noon and, unhindered by our convoy, travelled at full speed until evening, without encountering anyone in the woods. Moving to the right from our column, I traveled along local paths, across fields and through woods, largely guided by my instincts, apprehensive about the dangers of falling into the enemy's hands. By evening I reached a *folwark* where I fortunately found a good-hearted estate manager who fed me and, upon inquiring about my direction, informed me that I had deviated from the path. He gave

---

9 Nagaikas were leaded whips of great length and thickness that were particularly associated with the Cossacks.

me thorough directions on the road I had to take during the night and warned me to take precautions to avoid the French who were not far away. He even kept my tired horse and gave me a new one, on an understanding that I would claim her on my way back. It was good fortune itself that led me to this kind man. I do not know if I could have returned without his assistance. Having sustained myself with a dinner and a fresh horse, I resumed my race once again.

At first, the night was quite dark but as the moon rose in the sky, it cast its pale light on surrounding objects, presenting them in a deceptive form and frightening me with phantoms instead of showing me the way. I finally entered an empty village and noticed the figures of two horsemen moving at the end of a long street. Their movement caused me to immediately stop and turn to the closest yard, where I remained in the dark so as to conceal myself. The two dragoons soon passed by me but the poor moonlight prevented me from determining whether they were friends of foes. As the patrol departed, I quietly came out into the street and carefully moving next to the buildings, gradually accelerated my speed before finally galloping away from the road. After traveling for some three *verstas* [2 miles], I observed campfires in the distance, but I could not determine whether they were ours or the enemy's. So I moved off the road into the brushwood and cautiously proceeded forward, avoiding outposts and gradually approaching the campfires. At last, as I was about ten *sazhens* [70 ft.] away from the campfire, I recognized Cossacks by their long lances and conversation. I could not hide my satisfaction. I approached them so quietly that they did not notice me and immediately asked them whether they belonged to Dokhturov's corps. Receiving affirmative responses, I asked them to lead me directly to the general. The night was quiet and the clouds had concealed the moon. The troops seemed to have arrived just recently and the general himself was asleep in a barn. I was met by his adjutant, whom I handed the package to, and asked to wake up the general. Dokhturov woke up in front me, asked for a candle and, after reading the letter, said, "Look how concerned they have become. Tell them I am safe and sound. Doubelt, write them a response!" Doubelt, the adjutant, quickly went to a table to write the letter. I learned then that, during the last combat of the corps' rearguard on the Skvira River, the Mariupolskii Hussars had suffered losses trying to protect the train while it was crossing the pontoon bridge over the river, and that part of the train had been captured.

Exhaustion gradually prevailed over me. After travelling for over fifty *verstas* [33 miles], all at full speed, and riding such a long distance for the first time, I was completely drained. My head was burning and sleep kept overpowering me. While the adjutant wrote his letter and had it signed and sealed, I slept like a dead person, leaning against the table. But at the adjutant's first words, "Hey, it's ready!", I jumped up, took the letter, mounted the horse and galloped back along the same route that I came by. By dawn I had already reached the *folwark*, where I thanked the good-hearted estate manager for his help, took back my horse and resumed my trip.

At 8 a.m. on 25 June [7 July], I encountered the 4th Corps on its march from Gaidukovshizna. I dismounted in front of the Count just as he came out of the hut to mount his steed. Staggering from lack of sleep and extreme fatigue, I gave him the package. The always austere Count gave an amiable and benevolent glance, read the letter and told me, "Go ahead and take some rest, and then stay with me." But where was I supposed to go to rest if everyone was marching? Of the physical hardships I experienced, sleep deprivation was the worst. My horse was worn out and I felt as if I was broken into pieces, I went into the woods and lay down on a small meadow, wrapping the bridle around my hand and giving way to sleep just as everyone else was waking up. My horse insatiably ate the grass near my head and this noise, like the flow of a stream, soothed my long-desired slumber.

I slept like dead for about two hours until I felt the sun beating down on my head. The sun shone brightly in the azure sky and its rays made the tips of the tall birches golden. My horse stood nearby, with his head bowed and napping. A dull silence reigned all around me. Rejuvenated by sleep, I freshened myself and mounted my trusted steed, which slowly began to trot carrying me forward. As we traveled, we passed by some exhausted troops who were resting on stumps near a puddle. After traveling for about fifteen *verstas* [10 miles], I caught up with the infantry of the 4th Corps, which was marching through a village. Seeing the horses belonging to Count [Osterman-Tolstoy's] suite in front of a local nobleman's mansion, I tied my horse to the fence next to the other horses, and entered the house. In the middle of the room there was a large table with the remnants of a hastily eaten breakfast: overturned glasses, empty bottles, a sauce spilled all over the table cloth, spilled salt and bread crusts; all that was left was a dish with a piece of *bishka*[10] and another with some fried chicken. Three decently dressed ladies with tearful eyes and handkerchiefs in their hands sat at large windows, gazing despondently at their guests, who mostly kept coming and going without paying any respect to them as if they owned the place. That said, stroking their mustaches and jingling their spurs, some of the younger hussars and adjutants from Count [Osterman-Tolstoy's] retinue tried to entertain the ladies so as to soothe their grief and unwittingly entice poignant smiles from them.

Entering the front room, I made a slight bow to those present and, being very hungry after a difficult trip, I happily treated myself to some *bishka*. Checking bottles, I found some remaining liquid in one of them and drank it down, only to discover that it was extremely acidic and only remotely comparable to wine. All of us then mounted our horses, bid farewell to our hospitable hostesses and, leaving them to the mercy of providence and the French, we rode away to catch up with the Count, who had already left, deep in his thoughts.

In the evening, at the camp at Novoselki, I met my comrades-in-arms from my company, told them about my remarkable journey,

---

10 Bishka - animal joints.

and, for all that I was in a bivouac tent, spent as a lovely night in as if I were sleeping on a couch back at home.

The following day I was given a new horse and ordered to rejoin the Count's entourage. Yet his aides, orderlies and other dandies in beautiful, patterned uniforms, and on swift horses, looked snobbishly at me, wearing a blackened collar and riding an old nag with a modest Cossack saddle. I felt uncomfortable here, having no comrades and feeling rather bored. Finally, after the Count did not ask for me for an entire day, I decided to leave his suite without telling anyone and return to my comrades, thinking that if I were needed, I would certainly be called upon. And so the ball was over.

In the evening of 27 June [9 July], our troops entered the fortified camp on the Dvina. The battery was assigned a place on a slope above the river at the edge of the left wing, but the green rye around us was so tall that we could not see anything in front of us. The 4th Corps and 2nd Cavalry Corps encamped on the left flank, behind the last few redoubts.

The fortified camp on the Dvina was prepared before the start of the campaign, and thus our intention to retreat there must have been known to Napoleon, who could take necessary measures to separate our forces. This camp was, in many respects, similar to the one [Tsar] Peter I [the Great] had at Poltava [in 1709]. At Poltava, a river and steep ravines were located behind the camp so that the Russians had no alternative but to fight to the death or gain victory; here also there was a major river with steep banks, but three large bridges, protected with entrenchments, had been built to allow the troops to escape in case of a setback. At Poltava, there had been places to the fore that were covered in woods and fortified with redoubts; here, too, there was a forest, while *abatis* had been constructed on the left flank and ten redoubts were built in front of the camp. Finally, at both places, a single battle was intended to decide the salvation or destruction of one of the warring armies. Judging from the major efforts and expenses spent on building extensive fortifications at the

Dvina camp, we can certainly assume that the commander-in-chief intended to fight a decisive battle there. Yet his intention was not fulfilled. Maybe Napoleon avoided engaging us at the Dvina camp on account of the fate that had befallen the hero of Sweden [King Charles XII at Poltava] or maybe he fighting his way through barren provinces toward our northern capital formed no part of his plan, but, whatever the reason, in the fact is that he chose not to advance to the Dvina camp and left us alone.

Sheltered by the redoubts, we at least had the advantage of resting in peace for a few days. The commander-in-chief [Barclay de Tolly] expected the arrival of the 2nd [Western] Army, which was supposed to march through Vileika and Minsk. But its route was lengthier than the 1st Army's. Furthermore, at the start of our retreat, Napoleon launched a strategic maneuver to divide our armies, sending Marshal Davout with troops in between our forces. We had good reason to worry about the survival of Prince Bagration…

The day of our entry into the Dvina camp marked the anniversary of the famous battle of Poltava. To mark the occasion, an Imperial order was issued which revived the Russian soldiers' spirits that began to waver because retreating was so uncustomary to them. The order declared, "Until the reunion of our armies, it was necessary by a momentary and indispensable retreat to restrain your ardor to check the insolent advance of the enemy. But a new occasion now arises to manifest your tried valor and to gather the recompense for the labors you have endured." After this order, everyone was determined to wait for the enemy [at the Dvina camp]. The hearts of Russian soldiers filled with courage again and they reminded each other about the battle of Poltava, while everyone was ready to emulate their ancestors' glorious example on the banks of the Dvina.

The rumors claimed that our forces had spread a proclamation to the French and German troops via the enemy outposts. The former were told that they were blind instruments of a man with unlimited and insatiable ambition, while the latter were reminded of the humiliation that they endured in the service of the conqueror of their fatherland. If we had indeed released such a proclamation with the intention of undermining the enemy's morale, it is unlikely that it would have had any effect: the French were dazzled by the glory of Napoleon for as long as his eagles brought victories to them, while the Germans were so convinced of the impregnability of his power and so afraid of his vengeance, that no offers could tempt them.

Meanwhile, we held religious services throughout the camp to thank the Lord for granting a victory to Ataman Platov at Mir, where he had routed the Polish cavalry.[11] Who could look into the future and glean the secrets of our destinies? Our prolonged withdrawal, which was unusual for Russians, and the memories of continued French victories during the last campaign [in 1806-1807] inadvertently affected the fortitude of our soldiers. In candid conversations they often invoked the glorious names of [Peter] Rumyantsev and [Alexander] Suvorov.[12] During religious service and prayers, the Russian soldiers, hitherto so confident in their valor, stood solemnly with downcast gazes, as if confessing their impotence and hoping only for divine help to protect their beloved homeland, while, such was the solemnity of the moment that one and all prayed with reverent fervor, many with tears in their eyes.

Matvei Ivanovich Platov's victories not only pleased the men but also enlivened them with hope for future success. They told each other, "Here at least is one fellow who still beats the French in Russian style!" I must note that the soldiers, in a special sign of respect for the Cossack Ataman, called him not by his last name but always by his first and patronymic names.

---

11 The combat at Mir took place on 9 and 10 July; the Cossacks thrashed the Polish lancers and gained the first major Russian victory in the war.

12 Rumyantsev and Suvorov were the foremost Russian commanders of the 18th century, whose victories over the Poles and the Turks (and in the case of Suvorov, the French in 1799) had become the epitome of the Russian military glory.

THE RUSSIAN CAMPAIGN OF 1812

While we remained at the Dvina camp, we received news that the French army was already suffering from a major lack of supplies. Indeed, marching in our wake, they certainly would have been desperate for provisions. As we abandoned the countryside to the enemy, we intentionally devastated it to make it more difficult for the enemy to live off it: we mercilessly trampled the tall and dense green grains of various kinds. Our infantry, marching always in divisional columns on both sides of the road, left behind a wide trail of trampled and devastated grains. The army left entire stretches of land behind it that was scorched as if by terrible strikes of lightning. The land was always damp due to rain and dew and was therefore unhealthy for soldiers yet unaccustomed to life in the field, so the straw from roofs of the abandoned villages was gathered for bedding, and all the fences, doors, and shutters broken up to be used as firewood. Whatever was left after the soldiers' departed was then burnt by the Cossacks. Wherever he went, the enemy only found complete devastation in our wake. Roads and dams were damaged, while, even at this best time of the year, nature, the frenzies of nature assisted us in harming the enemy as the heavy rain flooded anywhere that was marshy and low-lying. All of this delayed the movement of the enemy forces, especially his artillery and supply trains.

Our men and horses endured these hardships better than the enemy since they were born in this peculiar climate and were better accustomed to rough life. The gentle French, Germans, and Italians must have felt that they had entered the land of their own demise. Our soldiers only suffered from unbearable summer heat. During our long marches, wearing heavy knapsacks, shakos and thick woolen clothes, our young soldiers quickly grew tired. At every puddle of water, they rushed with their canteens to scoop up some warm dirty water which they drank eagerly, without ever succeeding in quenching their thirst. Exhausted, they often fell behind their regiments, went aside to lay down somewhere to rest, and then fell into the hands of the enemy. Although the rearguard was required to pick up straggler, it quite often faced difficult circumstances that prevented it from doing so, and, during the retreat, our army must have suffered sizeable losses as a result.

From June 27 [9 July] to July 2 [14], we rested safely inside the Dvina camp. There was no news about the enemy's movements, which encouraged our troops as they thought that the French, exhausted by their marches, had already become equal to us in numbers and did not dare to attack us in our fortifications. Thanks to the government's assiduousness, we suffered no shortage: the troops received their rations of meat and [fortified] wine, while horses got oats, and sutlers provided officers with tea, sugar, and wine. Evenings were marked with sunset parades and music. Soldiers built decent huts where officers also found enough space to lie down. Merry comradeship cast aside impending dangers to the fatherland. Days were clear and nights cool. Laying under coats and admiring stars in the nightly sky, we fell asleep in calm complacency, periodically awakened by loud calls, in various voices, of sentries standing guard around the camp, and this wild harmony reminded us that we were indeed at war.

Chapter III

From the Dvina to Smolensk

In vain we waited for Napoleon. It seemed that he and his troops had been resting as well. If he had pushed onwards with his maneuver aimed at separating our armies, he might have had time to intercept us at Vitebsk and force the 1st Army to embark on a much longer route in order to join with the 2nd Army. Waiting for Napoleon, we learned that his columns proceeded by us in the direction of Polotsk. Thus, we had to leave the Dvina camp and hurry to join the 2nd Army at Vitebsk where, everyone thought, it would arrive without a fail.

On 2 [14] July, the 1st Army began to cross the Dvina: the infantry moved across two pontoon bridges while the artillery crossed on *platschuits*.[1] All three bridges were protected by a large *tête-de-pont*. The crossing was conducted in a proper manner but the presence of a large number of transport vehicles on the opposite bank created a backlog that slowed movement. The deep sandy ground between the pine woods also complicated our movements. Had the enemy arrived and opened fire, we would not have crossed this river without loss but, as it turned out, we moved safely across. The 4th Infantry Corps, along with the 3rd [Infantry] Corps, moved to the other side of a sandy road that ran through the woods but we only managed to reach the village of Yustinovo. The following day, the 1st Army marched in two columns upstream along the Dvina River: the left column consisted of the 2nd and 5th Infantry Corps, while the right column included the 3rd and 4th Corps. Count Wittgenstein's 1st Corps was

---

1 A Dutch term for a flat-bottomed wide boat that was used to transport heavy cargo on rivers, as well as used to construct temporary bridges.

left behind to protect the approaches to St. Petersburg, The Dvina River separated us from the enemy and that day we bivouacked in battle order near the village of Prudniki.

On 6 [18] July, at noon, we marched to Polotsk. The large stone buildings attracted attention as we passed by. Local residents could not be seen and only rarely did anyone appear in town. A dull emptiness reined everywhere and only the sound of artillery passing, horses neighing and soldiers' combative voices could be heard as they marched in dense columns. Accompanying my guns, I listened to a conversation between our cannoniers. One said, "It seems the cursed one [Napoleon] has tremendous forces. Look how much land was given to him for free, almost all of old Poland, and now this city will be his as well."[2] "We will see," - said the other cannonier – "maybe he is intentionally being lured this far." "Intentional or not, all of this is certainly unprecedented. Who has ever run away so far without a fight and to surrender so much for free! After all, as we leave these lands, the Polcs will rise up, support [Napoleon] and triple his forces." "Keep running your mouth," replied the old bombardier. "It seems they did not ask for your opinion!" Others laughed. Meanwhile, on the other side of the cannon I saw a civilian in a blue coat, who approached one of our caissons and, in a low voice, asked the driver, "Listen, how many charges do you have in this box?" "Why are you asking?" the artilleryman brusquely replied. "He is a spy!" I shouted, "Hold! Catch him!" Our cannoniers rushed after him but he ducked into an alley and disappeared.

After marching about three *verstas* [2 miles] away from the city, we bivouacked once again in battle formation. The infantry was deployed in two lines, artillery was positioned on the flanks and

---

2 As the result of the three Polish Partitions, Russia destroyed the Polish-Lithuanian Commonwealth and acquired vast tracts of lands to the west. In 1793, the Second Partition transferred to Russia the major remnant of Lithuanian Belorussia and the western Ukraine, including Podolia and part of Volhynia, while two years later, the Third Partition, gave Russia all Polish-Lithuanian territory east of the Neman (Nieman) River, and the rest of the Volhynian Ukraine.

between regiments. The commander-in-chief's headquarters moved with our column.

The following day we bivouacked behind the village of Ostrovlyany, north of the Dvina. At that moment nature presented us with all of its charm. The setting sun gilded the hills and trees, the clear waters of the Dvina reflected the azure of heaven and quietly flowed between the lofty banks, attracting our attention by their refreshing coolness; the dense and bright green trees were so burdened with leaves that their branches bent toward the water and seemed to be absorbing the life-giving moisture. The air was full of fragrance from flowers that pleased our senses. Leaving the camp to take a stroll, I went to the river, lay down on the green bank overlooking the water and quietly admired nature. My sentimentality was deeply affected as I fixed my gaze on the distant shore, gradually sinking into a romantic reverie. Seeing the birds chasing one after the other while hiding in bushes, I told myself, "Nature breathes with love and disperses her gifts for the enjoyment of man and yet what does man aspire to do? To exterminate his own kind, to destroy public welfare..." Unfamiliar sadness crushed my heart, and my spirit seemed to have left the hostile world of men for the wonderful world of fantasy; I imagined a charming garden, where I heard the sound of a harp and the gentle voice of a singer. In the distance across the river, I saw agile Nymphs playing with flowers... their gay laughter resounding in echoes... But what was happening? Alas, these were soldiers who had come clattering along with their kettles to get some water for their gruel! So farewell, my dear ghosts of fantasy. I suddenly felt the reality of my cheerless existence, sighed deeply and went back to the camp.

On 10 [22] July, we moved to the village of Staroe. Our artillery had to deploy near a tavern. It was raining heavily and having no tents, we sought shelter at a Jew's house, but it was locked. Axes were quickly produced [and doors broken] – and the interior of a temple suddenly revealed itself to us. Thrilled to find shelter, we camped in an empty tavern as well as we could. Each of us took up his own spot: some on a bench, others by a stove or inside the Jew's bedroom. We brought some hay in and spread a carpet – such a good apartment we had not had since Vilna, and by now we had had enough of bivouacs. A samovar was set up; we sat in a circle, smoked some tobacco, drank tea, dried off and got cheery. Everyone did what he desired. One prankster found an old wardrobe that belonged to the Jew, dressed himself up and presented himself as a Jew at prayer; another one dressed himself as a Jewess and flirted with us. We laughed. But this marketplace entertainment soon bored our eminent commanders and they disappointed the Jew and the Jewess.

We soon witnessed another rather charming scene. On the eve of the war, a young physician was assigned to our brigade. He brought his beautiful young wife with him, a sentimental German girl. To see such a beauty during the march, there is something particularly attractive in it for both single and married men because her single glance set you on fire, rekindling animal magnetism. Now, in this rainy weather the poor physician did not know what to do with his pretty wife. He had nothing except for a chaise but anyone can get bored living forever inside the chaise, and in such crowded conditions. We remembered the beautiful woman and to preserve her health, we suggested that the physician stay with us, in the company of honorable gentlemen, while the poor weather lasted. Humility and modesty made the woman hesitant to accept the offer, but the need to rest in a safe refuge soon overcame her timidity. The spouses whispered something to each other, held hands and seemed to have agreed not to separate, imagining perils in our company. They came in and sat down together. She was offered tea, while the physician was given *punsch* – one glass after another. Questions ensued, followed by answers and another round of questions – the [drunk] physician was gradually separated from his wife and put to bed. Now (and no, dear reader, it is not what you think happened) all the young men began to buzz around the smiling, rosy-cheeked German girl like bees around a rose... Some sighed, others were beside themselves from some kind of magnetic or galvanic effect that the woman's looks had on them... One is quite curious how this situation would have ended but a pot of gruel and pans with a *bishk* were suddenly ushered into the room. We moved from the ideal to the material and sat down to dine just as the sun was going down. The smell of food tickled our sleeping physician's nose, and the sound of tin plates and spoons touched his ear. As he woke up, he suddenly remembered his wife and rushed to find her. And so, these two sat together smiling out of joy and eating a Russian soup from a shared cup. Thus, the tavern gave us a good night's rest, dry shelter, joyous company and plenty of food as we enjoyed this luxury with the beautiful woman. We spent the entire night dreaming sweet dreams.

The following evening, the 1st Army's three infantry corps (3rd, 4th and 5th) and one cavalry corps crossed the Dvina River at Vitebsk and deployed in battle formation near the Luchesna River, on a field in front of the road to Babinovichi. Crossing the Dvina River cheered our soldiers and, as we deployed, they thought about fighting the enemy. Each of them burned with eagerness to finally engage the enemy and to show the French that we were not fleeing from them defeated. Realizing the danger that hung over our Fatherland, none of us thought about our lives, but each was willing to die or shed the enemy's blood to wash away the humiliation that this retreat had covered Russian arms with.

Closing [the distance] with the enemy seemed to set the stage for a most terrible battle. Soldiers thought that the fight would begin if not today, then certainly tomorrow. They cheered the news that a certain cornet of the Life Guard Uhlan Regiment, while out on patrol duty, had led his squad against a picket of French Red Lancers and, having killed some of them, captured 30 men.

At 2 a.m. on 13 [25] July, our 4th Corps, which included no more than 8,000 men, was ordered to advance along the left bank of the Dvina toward the village of Ostrovno before sunrise. This corps was reinforced by a dragoon division, Life Guard Hussar and Sumskii

Hussar Regiments, and a company of horse artillery. In total, there were approximately 11,000 men under command of Count Osterman-Tolstoy.

Our commander-in-chief was determined to repulse the enemy attacks from this [northern] direction so as to allow for an unimpeded union with the 2nd Army. It seemed, therefore, that he was ready to give battle. At dawn, we broke camp. The soldiers crossed themselves to ensure a good start, and moved forward with resolution. As soon as we reached the Ostrov road, we heard the sound of gunfire at some distance from Vitebsk. Our advance guard was already in action. The Life Guard Hussars charged the French outpost near a local tavern and became so inspired by this success that they hurried in pursuit of the fleeing six horse-artillery cannon. But the French expected them to do so, and they soon counterattacked with superior forces, sabering some of our hussars, chasing them back and reclaiming all six guns. The Nezhinskii Dragoons arrived just in time to help the hussars, while the Sumskii Hussar and 1st Jäger Regiments successfully contained further enemy attacks.

As we approached the site of the combat, we saw the returning Leib-Hussars in their beautiful uniforms and shakos bearing the Imperial arms, and on handsome gray horses. They rode with reigns lowered, covered in dust, some with bandaged arms, others with bloody faces. The sight of these wounded men caused much consternation in our hearts, which, however, drew comfort in seeing wounded Frenchmen, six men who were marched away into captivity by the Nezhinskii Dragoons. I studied these terrible foes with great curiosity, in their blue and red trousers, without coats, with thick locks of braided hair covered in fat hanging to their napes; these men were tall and healthy – dragoons. Their lurching movements revealed considerable fatigue while sweat, mixed with dust, disfigured their faces. Some of them had saber cuts on their cheeks, which were covered in coagulated blood, while others sustained injuries to their arms; but they all looked at us rather cheerfully and without despair.

THE RUSSIAN CAMPAIGN OF 1812

The closer we came to the battlefield, marching along the side of the main road, the clearer we heard the sound of gunfire. About one *versta* [0.66 miles] from the battlefield, we were ordered to stop and prepare for battle. Infantrymen began loading their muskets and the rattle of ramrods soon filled the air; artillerymen prepared ammunition, while officers drew their swords. The road was littered with helmets from our dragoons, broken swords and uniform flaps. The wounded, bloodied and hobbling jagers occasionally passed by but there was still no sight of corpses. The sense of a nearby battle, the first one in my life, took over. I still had no clear idea about what a battle was. I believed that everyone converging on a battlefield was destined to perish, that each cannonball and bullet would invariably kill or wound a man and therefore I would probably not survive this fight. But, seeing how bravely everyone around me marched onwards, I had no other choice but to follow their example. And so, I sat deep in thought on my gun carriage, observing everything around me with great attention. Passing by me, our artillery brigade commander saw me sitting quietly on a gun carriage and said: "Keep resting lad; the real work will soon begin." These were his last words because, as soon as he reached the battlefield, an enemy cannonball shattered his chest and, traversing through it, melted both his heart and gold coins that were inside his pocket.

Soldiers prepared for battle and bravely marched to face their death, which, it seemed they eagerly desired. Our company moved in between the Kexholmskii and Pernovskii Regiments from the 11th Division; its commander General Bakhmetyev I and Brigadier General Choglokov rode ahead of us. We were followed by the second brigade (Yeletskii and Polotskii Regiments) of the 11th Division, behind which moved the 23rd Division under General Bakhmetyev II, deployed in closed divisional columns. Our infantry moved rather quickly. When the cannonballs began to whistle above our heads and cut men from our ranks, the infantry rushed forward while the artillery trotted behind; the skirmishers scattered in brushwood, batteries were set up and the fight ensued.

FROM THE DVINA TO SMOLENSK

Ten guns of the 3rd Light Company turned right from the road and, having quickly unlimbered, began to fire. The enemy batteries engaged us from three sides; their cannonballs hopped all around us like rabbits. Dead soldiers lay on the road: one of them had his head torn off; another had his stomach ripped apart while a third lay without legs. My heart convulsed at their sight and an uncomfortable feeling took over. I became faint hearted and felt weakness in my knees. I was still deployed with my two guns on the road, without engaging in the firefight, when a colonel rode up to me and told me to take position on the left side of the roadway, pointing me toward a slight elevation. It was then that I woke up from my numbness, which lasted a few minutes.

Meanwhile, the Kexholmskii and Pernovskii Regiments marched off the road, one to the right and the other to the left; both units deployed along the edge of the woods in order to support the skirmishers who had scattered in front of them, and to protect our artillery. The Yeletskii Regiment was deployed in line next to the left flank of the Pernovskii Regiment. A murderous cannonade continued to intensify on both sides.

Veteran soldiers observe that fear disturbs the heart of a young soldier only before a battle begins because his thoughts still consider the deathly horrors that leave a bad impression. Once he is in the midst of battle, fear is eclipsed by rage. As he puts his life in danger, a soldier [ceases to be an observer and] becomes an active participant, and death ceases to frighten him. His heart fills with blood and he disregards danger, turning into a seemingly insensitive being. A person seemingly leaves the confines of ordinary existence; his physical body becomes restless while all manifestations of the soul are strained. I was in such a condition when our cannons were ordered to deploy at the designated spot. Suddenly cannonballs began to whistle by me: one of them hit a horse artilleryman while another sheared off a cannonier's legs together with his cartridge pouch; he fell in front of me and wretchedly cried, "Save me, Your Honor!"

Moments earlier I shuddered at seeing the dead but I became callous and simply ordered [my men] to drag him to the side so he did not interfere with our operations.

My two guns were deployed against three enemy cannon. I aimed both my guns at one enemy cannon and damaged it on the very first try through a ricochet shot. Upon seeing the French withdrawing the damaged gun, our soldiers cheered with shouts of "Hurrah!" As the number of cannon became equal on both sides, we engaged each other with equal success. The enemy cannonballs, hitting close to my guns, showered us with soil, while their grenades exploded in the air with a hellish scream. Noticing that the French maintained rather precise fire at my guns and had already killed another cannonier, I moved ten paces forward and most of the murderous enemy cannonballs began to fly over our heads; but, on the other hand, they now claimed entire ranks among the infantry that were deployed behind us. To replace the damaged cannon, the French deployed two more cannon and then opened a ferocious fire with their four cannon against my two. In the deafening din of cannonade and gunpowder I kept losing my concentration. The enemy cannonballs mercilessly ravaged the infantry behind me. So I decided to repay them by turning my fire against the enemy columns that had been moving forward along the main road. My cannoniers moved the cannon to the right and fired ricochet shots so successfully that they immediately disordered the enemy infantry and forced it to halt. General Choglokov, who was standing nearby in front of the [infantry] line, noticed my actions. He called me over to thank me for the successful operation of my artillery. Encouraged, I returned to my guns eager to get back in action when my cannoniers suddenly shouted, "Your Honor, cavalry! Look, in the brushwood!" Indeed, I saw a line of red hussars, approaching at a trot, who were half hidden by the bushes. Just as I issued orders to load the cannon with canister, an enemy cannonball struck the wheel of one gun, causing it to capsize; so we had to drag it back. Meanwhile, Major Tishin of the Yeletskii Regiment galloped to our position and asked me to hurry the remaining gun to the left flank of our line, where we had no reinforcements to counter cavalry.

This happened just as French General Ornano led his light cavalry in an attack, on both sides of the road, toward our line. I rushed after the major with the gun. In front of our line, our skirmishers scattered in the shrubs, doing their best to resist but the red hussars were already surrounding them; the jagers, firing in all directions, were gathered together. As soon as I brought my cannon alongside the infantry line, I saw a squadron of brave French hussars turn left and rush at our skirmishers with their sabers drawn; our entire infantry line opened a battalion volley while I fired canister. The entire enemy squadron was scattered: many fell from their horses while others ran back, our skirmishers were saved. Thus, the first of the French attacks was unsuccessful.

Meanwhile, my gunners had run out of ammunition. I took a caisson horse and galloped to find our company commander to ask him for a new cannon and ammunition. But alas, I was astounded by the condition of our artillery on the right side of the road! Several guns were scattered around, damaged or overturned, and dead gunners and horses lay among them. Forming a central battery, our company was ravaged by enemy cannonballs from three sides. The French cavalry then charged and, overcoming the canister fire of our entire battery, burst through the guns, sabering gunners, capturing an officer and almost getting away with two guns. But the Kexholmskii Regiment repulsed the French here as admirably as the Yeletskii and Pernovskii Regiments did on the left flank. I found our lieutenant colonel amidst great commotion. Upon seeing me, he asked, "You are still alive?!" "As you can see, just give me a gun and ammunition." – "What else, lad?" he continued, "Our entire company is shattered. Goryanov is captured; Schlippenbach and Braiko have lost their legs." The lieutenant colonel then approached Count Osterman and began to report to him that the company lost many men killed, and that there were quite a few damaged cannon that could no longer be employed.

THE RUSSIAN CAMPAIGN OF 1812

"What will you command of me, Your Grace?" he finally inquired. The count, sniffing tobacco, replied curtly, "Fire from those cannon that are still functional." Meanwhile, someone informed the count that the enemy cannonballs were claiming many lives in the infantry and suggested moving them back to safety. "[No!] Hold ground and die!" the Count sternly replied. A third aide soon approached and wanted to say something to the count when a cannonball ripped off his hand, which flew by the count. The officer fell from the horse, which was in an agitated state. "Take care of him," said the count, and turned his horse. This unshakable presence of mind in a commander at a moment when everything was in disarray all around him, was a genuine manifestation of the Russian character, embittered, as it was, by the disaster that struck its Fatherland. Looking at him, we all gained courage from his example and returned to our places, ready to die.

I found a caisson, brought it back to my cannon and resumed firing. I was soon reinforced by an ensign with two field guns, so we could eagerly return fire on the much larger enemy battery. The cannonade soon resumed with new ferocity along the whole line. Facing our determined defense, the French, of course, thought that we were continually reinforced by considerable forces from behind the woods, in front of which our troops were deployed on both sides of the road. To better reconnoiter our position, their generals moved forward along the main road on our left flank. I immediately issued orders to aim a cannon at them and our gunners fired the first shot so successfully that it landed right in the middle of the group of generals, scattering them in all directions; several staff-officers approached our cannon and praised the gunners for their action. I was pleased to see the damage my cannon caused the enemy: these last being men who willingly or not had become our foes, this is the only time when a man is allowed to enjoy the evil that he inflicts on fellow humans. I diligently aimed the cannon for another salvo, and, just as I stepped back to see how well the sight was set, an enemy cannonball suddenly appeared as a black dot in the sky and flew toward me out of the dense smoke. It should have been a death blow, but my inner sense or instinct of self-preservation had been enough to push me towards the cannon. Even so, the cannonball knocked me over. Soldiers rushed to me and, placing me on their muskets, carried me behind the front line. I thought that my legs had been blown off and dared not look at them. Just as the soldiers entered the forest, a most terrible musket fire began against enemy cavalry along our entire line. The soldiers, who carried me, thought that the French were close by, so they left me in the woods and quickly returned to their positions.

I thought my right leg was shattered around my foot area but I could still lean on my left leg. So I found a thick branch to prop myself up and, standing up with some difficulty, I slowly hobbled toward the road. I saw a terrible commotion there: drunk enemy lancers had broken through our line across the road and reached as far as our supply train, where they had caused great disorder before falling victim to their own arrogance since they could not find their way out. I came across the crawling and wounded (in the leg) old *Feuerwerker* Osipov, who, upon seeing me moving slowly out of the forest, cried with tears in his eyes, "Ah! Sir! You are still alive. Those damn Radziwill lancers slew everyone here!" I learned from this kind soldier that the drunken lancers had charged, for the second time, through our canister fire, broke into our battery, and indiscriminately cut down or smashed everything they encountered: men, horses, wheels, carriages; they had even scraped cannon with their swords. The soldier told me that the lancers were waving their sabers so senselessly that *Feuerwerker* Maximov threw one of them to the ground by striking him with a ramrod. The Kexholmskii and Pernovskii Regiments again repelled the French and saved our battery. A musket bullet had struck my *feuerwerker* in a thigh, so deep that it reached the bone. Leaning on my branch, I helped him to stand up and gave him another stick to lean on. We then went forward together, limping, groaning, and dragging ourselves to our supply train. The battle, meanwhile, raged all around us. Throughout this journey, I did not dare to look at my right leg and struggled to drag it along. Yet, the pain was intensifying, and soon it spread along my entire leg. I felt a burning sensation as if I was on fire. Reaching our supply train, I found our brigade paymaster, who advised me to get immediately onto a wagon that was evacuating Tutolmin, our divisional adjutant, who had been wounded: the poor lad had had his right arm ripped off above the elbow. Climbing onto the wagon, I finally decided to look at my foot, and was thrilled to see that only the rear side of my boot was broken and burnt as if by fire: the cannonball would have certainly severed my leg if not for my internal instinct that saved me. The cannonball clipped only the heel of my right leg, smashing the boot. Its blow was, however, rather strong, and I could not move the leg and had to keep it bent at the knee. With his forearm missing, Tutolmin's injury was much more serious than mine and he lay half-dead next to me. Meanwhile, the paymaster confirmed that Schlippenbach and Braiko had suffered leg wounds from shell fragments and that Senior Lieutenant Goryanov had been captured.

Our company suffered considerable losses in this battle: we lost up to sixty cannoniers and some 30 horses; four cannons had their carriages and wheels damaged; one officer was captured and three wounded. Yet our unit had survived two cavalry attacks and a crossfire sustained by several enemy batteries. The Polish lancers formed by Prince Radziwill had inflicted severe damage to us, but the prince himself was wounded during the attack when he was shot in the leg by our canister. On the eve of war, when we were quartered in Nesvizh, the prince had been a frequent visitor at our camp, attending training sessions in musketry and breaking camp, or carousing with our company commanders. We even visited his estate to attend two magnificent balls that he had organized. Who would have thought that circumstances would drive us so far apart, turning us into enemies and compelling us to inflict such destruction on each other?

FROM THE DVINA TO SMOLENSK

For our actions in this battle, the commander-in-chief [Barclay de Tolly], on Count Osterman's nomination, awarded us, three wounded officers, with the Order of St. Anna (4th class) to be affixed to our swords, while the company commanders were given the same order of the 2nd class to be worn around the neck.

As we expected, the first battle proved to be rather fierce and resolute. Count Osterman-Tolstoy had gallantly repelled the enemy's attacks, and thereby compensated for the initial setback our advance guard had suffered. In the evening, he then retreated beyond the woods. It so happened that during the first encounter of the two warring armies, our guard cavalry engaged Napoleon's guard cavalry, the Russian 4th Corps fought with the French 4th Corps, and Prince Radziwill charged with his lancers through the canister of our artillery that used to stay with him in Nesvizh. What a strange coincidence!

The hearse, on which I lay with Tutolmin, drove past the columns of the 3rd Infantry Division, deployed on either side of the road in support of Count Osterman's corps. A servant ran out from one of the houses and asked me: "Would you like some wine, sir?"

– "Who sent you?" – "My master." – "Thank him for his kindness but we do not have time to drink wine now." This generous gentleman offered this indulgence to all the wounded as he tried to be of some service to his countrymen. We were soon brought into town and placed inside a room in a tradesman's house. Tutolmin began to suffer from a fever. The town surgeons visited us in the evening. They cut and removed my boot; my right heel was deformed, swollen and turning blue. It burned as if it was inside a fire and touching it caused excruciating pain. But cold dressings reduced the inflammation. Tutolmin and I were both bandaged. Poor Tutolmin, weakened by the loss of blood and vital fluids, had to be prepared for a terrible operation: his arm was torn above the elbow and his wound dressings were hastily made on the battle field so the surgeons found it necessary to cut the protruding bone and pull his muscles together - in short, he had to be operated on. They reassured us that they would visit again tomorrow, which only increased our insomnia.

On 14 [26] July, just as General Konovnitsyn was fighting off the French near Peschanka, the town surgeons showed up as promised, and this time they brought their instruments with them. At that moment, I found them more terrifying than the French cavalry. The lead surgeon's blue coat, powdered wig and long nose appeared to me as nightmares for several nights in a row. The surgeons first turned to Tutolmin. They encouraged and caressed him, then gave him some drops, put him in a chair and began to unwrap his bandages. Sitting on my bed, I stared attentively at what was happening across the room. The cutters [*rezateli*] washed the wound, where one could see shreds of flesh hanging down and a sharp piece of bone protruding. The surgeon in a powdered wig took a curved knife out of the box, rolled up his sleeves to the elbow, quietly approached the shattered arm, suddenly grabbed it and turned the knife so swiftly and deftly that the hanging flesh fell down at once. Tutolmin screamed and began to moan but the surgeons began to talk loudly so as to drown out his moans with their noise. They used hooks to pull and hold fresh flesh and muscles while the surgeon cut off the bone. It clearly caused insufferable pain to Tutolmin who shuddered, groaned, endured agony and occasionally fainted; he was often sprinkled with cold water and allowed to sniff some alcohol. Once the bone was cut, the surgeons pulled the muscles into a lump and covered the wound with skin that was purposefully preserved and turned out; the wounded was then sewn up with silk, covered in a compressed bandage and wrapped in dressings - and so ended the operation. Tutolmin was laid to bed, half-dead.

The terrifying surgeon, in a powdered wig, with his sleeves rolled up and still holding a curved knife, then turned to me and apparently no longer willing to operate, he asked, "Well, how are you?" I was terrified and, hiding my foot, I replied, "I am doing well, Sir, there is no need to cut me." "Let us see!" he replied, and

FROM THE DVINA TO SMOLENSK

I did not dare to resist: my deformed heel was swollen and all blue; it seemed already covered with the *Antonov fire* [gangrene]. With the aid of glasses, the surgeons carefully examined it, then talked among themselves in Latin: the powdered wig seemed undecided whether to cut my leg or not; maybe he thought that my Achilles heel was damaged. I confess that at that moment, the esteemed surgeon, standing with his curved knife in front of me, seemed to be more terrifying than Napoleon and the French. I could read the sentence of life or death on his wrinkly forehead since I did not think my weak health would allow me to survive the operation. Fortunately, the unanimous verdict of the 'Latins' was that the curved knife should be set aside. That said a small pen-knife was suddenly waved in front of my face: it seemed that I was not going to avoid cutting after all. Turning me over, the surgeons grabbed my leg tight and suddenly struck my swollen heel with the knife. I screamed with pain, but then felt relieved: the wound was full of clotted blood that had accumulated under the skin, and it was it's bluish hue which had given it the appearance of Antonov fire and raised the surgeons' suspicion. Thus, my foot was spared after being so close to being severed from my body. I was thrilled that I was not left disabled, but I soon suffered from the high fever associated with such injuries and is caused by blood inflammation

In the morning while, we rested officers, some of them familiar to us and some of them not, came to see us and discuss the events of the battle. Everyone was excited that we had shown ourselves equal to the French and, that despite their [numerical] superiority, we still bravely repelled their attacks.

In the evening, when Tutolmin and I were alone, the house's owner, a commoner, entered the room. Jingling some coins in his hand, he asked, "Do you gentlemen have any silver? I would exchange them for as many banknotes as you want." – "Why do you need it?" – "Because new guests [the French] will soon visit us," he answered smiling – "and I will have to pay them off to save my soul and my little house" - "What an imbecile!" I replied. He sniggered and left. Every family has its black sheep, indeed.

On 15 [27] July our army stood in battle array on the right side of the Luchesna River, on open heights beyond the town. The right flank was protected by a large mass of cavalry while the left flank was anchored on the wooded heights. Because of the resolute Russian resistance over the preceding two days, Napoleon could assume that our commander-in-chief had finally decided to compete with him in military talent and good fortune. He could happily look forward to celebrating victory since he had up to 190,000 men, and could expect to crush our 90,000 and drown them in the Dvina. Believing that Prince Bagration's army would arrive in time to attack the French from the rear; and much impressed by the manner in which our eager troops had demonstrated their fury and gallantry during the preceding two days, our commander-in-chief [Barclay de Tolly] seemed ready to make a brave fight of it. But we suddenly received news that Prince Bagration had found Mogilev occupied by the French and, unable to capture it, turned to Stary Bykhov and Rogachev, where he intended to cross the Dnieper and join the 1st Army at Smolensk. This important news immediately caused the general movement of the army. In full daylight, our troops began to break their camps and depart through town. Deployed about five *verstas* [3.3 miles] from our main forces, the French could not see this movement, while, even if they had noticed it, they would certainly have considered it as an ordinary redeployment on the eve of a general battle. They did not expect us to retreat just after we had demonstrated such menacing intentions.

That same day, Tutolmin and I lay quietly in our room; we felt a bit better, though still rather weak for want of proper food: we could barely eat the disgusting broth that our orderlies brought us every day. I was suffering again from recurring fever but could at least sit next to the window and watch soldiers passing by in the street. However, the noise made by the retreating troops continued throughout the day and night, and it was only at dawn that Tutolmin and I managed to catch some sleep.

Napoleon was naturally surprised and furious when at dawn of 16 [28] July he could find no trace of our main army, or even of a single Cossack. The road into town was clear and open gates awaited him at the entrance to the abandoned town. Only seriously wounded and dead greeted his victorious army as it approached the town in triumph. During the night our rearguard managed to skillfully evade the enemy. The Russians had demonstrated on this occasion that they are as adroit at retreating when it is necessary as they are in attacking.

In the morning, a remarkable silence reigned over the town. There was not a single noise inside our home or in the streets. Bored, I got up and, seeing that it was a clear day, I sat next to the window: I could not imagine that our troops had completely abandoned the town and that the French were entering it unobstructed. I suddenly saw a few Cossacks riding by; a certain civilian official on a horse noticed my pale exhausted face, rode up to the window and asked me hurriedly, "Who's there?" - "Wounded" I replied - "What! You have not been evacuated yet…?" he retorted and disappeared. Five minutes later he appeared with two peasant carts and ordered us to get in and leave the town as soon as possible since the French were already at the gates. "What?" I marveled, "And where are our troops?" – "Sit down, sit down..." he replied and rode away.

With the help of some peasants (our orderlies had saved themselves earlier) we came out of the house and sat in separate carts that were each pulled by a pair of horses. Not a soul could be seen in the street – a mysterious and dreadful silence hung heavily in the air, occasionally disrupted by the groans of the wounded that were lying in different positions on the pavement; among these miserable souls, I noticed many gray Sumskii hussars as well as jagers.

Tutolmin being unable to travel fast because of the extreme pain that every bump caused him, I soon parted from him: I am unaware whether he survived or not . But my driver drove his old nags at a trot beyond the town and in the wake of the army. There I saw a few Cossacks and told the driver to slow down since I was feeling sick from the rough ride. After traveling for about 12 *verstas* [8 miles] on the road to Porechye, I saw troops bivouacked in battle array and immediately found my company. Everyone thought I was gone so they were surprised by my survival, which was a lucky one indeed: if I had not got up from the bed and stood by the window, I would have certainly fallen into the hands of the French.

I was told that the entire 1st Army was retreating to Smolensk, where it would join the 2nd Army. Our 4th Corps and the 2nd Corps comprised the left column. Meanwhile, my artillery company, after it suffered losses during the battle at Ostrovno, was replenished with people, horses and ammunition but not officers. So beside Lieutenant Colonel M***, there was only the paymaster, his brother, and sickly me: Staff Captain Figner was on a mission somewhere, while Schlippenbach and Braiko had been sent to a field hospital.

On 17 [29] July we reached Porechye. The troops halted in a valley in front of the town; bivouacs were quickly set up and comforting bonfires soon began to smoke between the shelters. The weather was humid and the night proved to be quite cold. I suffered from another serious recurrence [of fever] and was moved to the deceased Colonel Kotlyarov's carriage, which remained in the company's train.

The terrified residents of Porechye, with their entire families crying and in despair, ran away from the town, into the woods and in all directions. Their homes were filled with troops who ransacked everything for their bivouacs and only those buildings were spared where generals, regimental commanders and their staff were billeted. Three infantry corps – 2nd, 3rd and 4th – ended up together in this town and it was naturally quiet crowded.

The sight of destruction and human tragedy horrified me: we plundered property belonging to our fellow countrymen; objects surrounding me plunged me into a state of morose depression and miserable thoughts filled my head. I raved about treachery and traitors and my feverish mind imagined the abominable Napoleon as a supernatural being protected by infernal forces. I had visions of the red hussars, in bearskin hats, galloping straight at me with their swords drawn, as well as of skinny tanned Italian skirmishers, finding their way through brushwood like hyenas and aiming their deadly weapons at me... Thus, the horrors I experienced before seemed now so much livelier. I had to cover my face with my hands so as to avoid seeing these ghosts, shuddering at imagining the demise of Russia. Suffering from high fever, I could not make any observations for several days.

On 20 July [1 August], all our corps approached Smolensk on the right side of the Dnieper and deployed in battle formation on a high plain in sight of the city, facing Porechye where the enemy was expected to come from. The wounded were ordered to be sent to Dukhovshchina and I was to leave my company. I feared falling into unknown hands and declared that I had better chances of survival under the care of our company physician than a field physician whose field hospital had to treat hundreds of wounded. With the company, I felt like I was with family: each soldier commiserated and helped me as did the surviving officers. Until now I rode in a carriage that moved with the train but because the moving artillery kept disturbing me with its rattling and noise, I moved to a different cart and, taking a driver, traveled separate from the train. Taking advantage of clear weather, I stopped often to enjoy shade inside groves, near clear streams, or along the main road, and to rest on soft green ground, picking a few flowers and escaping my current condition for just a few moments. My driver, meanwhile, let his horse graze on grass and cooked porridge and fried mushrooms; I admired the sight of the flickering flame and assiduousness of my self-taught chef. Thus, without taking any medication and with just one more dressing of the wound, I soon began to feel relief. Maybe it was the fresh air, food or my own nature but these few days of rest cured my fever. I reached Smolensk on 22 July [3 August] in much better health, although still weak. I stayed with the train that was deployed behind the army, above the Dnieper and in front of the city. About two *verstas* [1.2 miles] away I could see bivouacs and could hear a rumbling noise coming from the same direction while across the Dnieper I observed the city with gold-domed churches and white-stone houses, surrounded by an ancient wall, as if in one of the panoramas. I could see incessant activity on the road between the town and the army, with people and wagons constantly moving back and forth. In good weather I usually left the cart on crutches and sat on a carpet spread on the ground, admiring the vicinity, the sights of a military camp and city, reading books and writing in my campaign notebooks. I spent six days in this fashion Fresh air, freedom and tranquility proving to be stronger healing potions for me than any hospital could have been, I felt better day by day, and my wound slowly healed.

The rumors claimed that Ataman Platov and his Cossacks had crossed the river below the city to join the 1st Army and cover its left flank. I soon learned that the entire 2nd Army had arrived at Smolensk on the left side of the Dnieper. All of us were thrilled with joy, especially because we, out of ignorance, thought that Prince Bagration's army had perished. The Russians grew inspired once more, the united forces of our Orthodox warriors instilling each soldier with confidence that victory would finally be ours at the walls of Smolensk, and that the conqueror's ambition would finally be restrained and our continuous retreat finally brought to an end. The name of Bagration, who was so well-known for his courage, inspired hope in our troops. I shared these common expectations and, in fact, was so confident of our success that in a letter to my father, who lived in the Yaroslavl province, I wrote, among other things: "Our troops have retreated to Smolensk; perhaps we will go even further. But Bog-rati-on [the God of the Army] is with us and we will be in

FROM THE DVINA TO SMOLENSK

Paris soon!" At that time, every Russian believed that Bagration's name contained some mysterious power like the apocalyptic name of Napoleon, as a kind of good spirit against the demon.

After the retreat, which lasted nearly two months, our troops needed rest and fresh food. Rumours claimed that the enemy army was suffering deficiencies in everything, and was exhausted from never-ending marches through devastated country. Such news thrilled us. The rumors claimed that there was unrest in Napoleon's army, that his troops were no longer willing to march any deeper into the land of the Scythians. But the haughtiness and arrogance of those Frenchmen we captured certainly did not confirm it. They were far from being discouraged, and instead told us that we would all soon suffer their fate [of falling into captivity]; such was their confidence in the invincibility of Napoleon.

The retreat of our two armies from the borders of the Empire to Smolensk allowed the enemy to seize a vast territory, some 800 *verstas* [528 miles] wide, almost without a fight. The entire provinces of Vilna, Grodno, Minsk, and Courland, and parts of Belorussia and Smolensk province were occupied by Napoleon's troops. The 1st Army had covered, without much effort, nearly 550 *verstas* [360 miles] in nearly 30 days, excluding the rest at the Dvina camp. On the other hand, the 2nd Army had to conduct forced marches from Grodno to Mogilev, a distance of 650 *verstas* [430 miles] in just 18 days, or about 35 *verstas* [23 miles] per day. No matter how strong the Russian spirits were, their physical strength was sapped from continuous exertion; the difficult route through sands and marshes, which the 2nd Army had to take, wore the soldiers out and left considerable numbers of fatigued stragglers to fall into the hands of the enemy. Russia will always be grateful to the military talents of Prince Bagration, who showed an exemplary prudence in escaping traps that were set for him and in skillfully leading his army to Smolensk.

After their union, our two armies comprised about 120,000 men. Napoleon, meanwhile, had about 200,000 men between Vitebsk and the Dnieper River. Though he had tried to carry out his outstanding plan to divide our army, the emperor had failed to achieve his goal! In general, the human mind having no control over circumstances, only half of even the best designs of a commander are accomplished. And so it was that Napoleon's intention to split our armies was only partially successful. His failure must be credited to our generals, just as his success was dependent on the abilities of his generals who, however, acted indecisively.

Chapter IV

From Smolensk to Borodino

In consequence of the decision adopted by our generals, at the council of war, to attack an isolated enemy corps at Porechye, the combined forces of our two armies departed from their camp in the direction of Rudnya. This was the first offensive movement after a long retreat. The march itself was insignificant, but militarily it offered rather important opportunities and this alone was sufficient to revive the hopes of Russian soldiers in returning to the old habit of always advancing to the fore.

On 27 July [8 August] we learned that the French did not dare to go any farther, having taken position at Porechye, deployed in the forests behind the marshes and protected by *abatis*. This encouraged our soldiers; even as it was, they had already begun to perceive some of the beneficial consequences of retreating. Assuming that the enemy was exhausted by difficult marches and deprivation, we considered his apparent timidity as genuine. The superiority of the French, which seemed so terrifying to us, already appeared insignificant compared to the resilience of our Russian forces. It seemed that the Commander-in-Chief [Barclay de Tolly] was indeed eager to attack the enemy hidden in the woods at Porechye. After three days at the same place the troops became bored from idleness. We were thrilled to hear news of the first success of our offensive: it was said that Ataman Platov, with his Cossack advance guard, had fallen upon the French at Molevo Boloto, and captured a general, up to 30 officers and 500 soldiers. This news was received by everyone with enthusiasm, and no one doubted its veracity because every soldier then donned the menacing appearance of the defender of the Fatherland – everyone was a hero; victory seemed just a routine matter, and failure would have been unbelievable, even dishonorable.

An aggravated desire for Russian vengeance demanded not just a victory but the complete extermination of our enemies.

On 1 [13] August I returned to my company. I was partially recovered from my wound, which had not fully healed yet. My leg was wrapped in bandages and I used crutches to move around. I found my company deployed in the brush between the lines of infantry commanded by Staff Captain Figner, whom I had not seen since Swentsyan. Our previous company commander, Lieutenant-Colonel M., was transferred to another company to replace the deceased Colonel Kotlyarov. Lieutenant-Colonel M. was also given command of the brigade. The troops of the 2nd and 4th Corps were bivouacked near the village of Luscha and remained under the command of General of Cavalry Uvarov.

For the first time in my life I experienced the anxiety of camp life: the gypsy huts made of brushwood, hastily built and covered with grass, constituted our temporary shelters. Rain and cold night air forced us to constantly maintain bonfires in front of the huts and the smoke from wet firewood, mingled with tobacco fumes exhaled by smokers, burnt our eyes, tickled our throats, made us shed tears and cough. Our comrades, lounging on their coats on top of wet straw, entertained and amused themselves however they could. All the while I did not know what to do because of my injured leg. I felt awkward everywhere, suffered from pain and, as people say, all of this was not to my liking. It was then I began to pay closer attention to Figner. He loved to play at Boston and also games of *svaika*.[1] His face was always open, sometimes jovial but more often thoughtful. He spoke rapidly but quite eloquently. Although it is said that married officers and soldiers are softened by family life and for the most part

---

1 An old Russian game that involves throwing a large nail/spike into a ring laying on the ground.

lose their courage, Figner was an exception because he preserved his gallantry even while being married to a beautiful wife, whom he left in Pskov. But nature, it seems, has not been stingy in showering him with other gifts as well.

On 2 [14] August our troops marched forward 15 *verstas* [10 miles] deploying in a valley in front of Kasplya Lake. The fields were full of ripe grain that was so tall that it reached above soldiers' waists. Multicolored strands of grain caught our attention and we felt pity knowing that this scenic place would be trampled by soldiers pitching camp, thereby eradicating the fruits of the peasants' hard labor.

Meanwhile, as our troops went from place to place in front of Porechye, Napoleon prepared to deliver his counter blow against us by [launching a flanking attack] to threaten our rear. General Neverovskii's detachment,[2] deployed at Krasnyi, barely escaped destruction. The exceptional presence of mind and courage of this general saved the honor of Russian arms. Our troops fought their way through numerous enemies and although they suffered rather heavy casualties, none of them surrendered. We learned this during the night of 4 [16] August, after the French had already approached Smolensk.

At dawn on 4 [16] August, all of our troops marched hastily back to Smolensk. Regiments vied with each other as each regiment hurried to defend Smolensk, where we arrived during the evening after covering some 30 *verstas* [20 miles], nearly running the whole distance. We took position on the right bank of the Dnieper. The 4th Corps stopped to the right [west] of the city, below the suburbs. As we stood at the edge of the wood, we could hear a cannonade and thought the French had already taken the city. We were anxiously asking everyone we

---

[2] Bagration deployed this detachment at Krasnyi to guard against Napoleon's potential flanking movement. The detachment consisted of the 27th Infantry division, which was recently created from newly recruited infantry, and reinforced by substituting some of its units with more experienced regiments.

encountered about the fate of Smolensk, so important in terms of its location and so glorious because of its antiquity, the city upon which Russia always relied upon as its stronghold. Smolensk was always at the very heart of Russia. We were thrilled to hear that General Rayevskii repelled the French, who had attacked the Royal Bastion.[3] They had intended to capture the city to celebrate Napoleon's birthday and present it to the [Emperor]. Some said that, such was their celebratory mood, the French got drunk before assaulting the fortress. But the courageous General [Rayevskii], who had part of his troops inside the city, repelled the first attack by the audacious [French]. It was said that the French, after driving back the Cossacks and Neverovskii's detachment [on 14 August], even approached the city gates but were held up by a mere seven hundred soldiers of the train[4] led by a gallant major, before General Rayevskii arrived with his corps. The town had not suffered any damage yet and only the most affluent of the residents had departed from it.

5 [17] August proved to be fateful for the city and bloody for the contending armies. Before dawn, General Dokhturov's 6th Corps and General Konovnitsyn's 3rd Division replaced Rayevskii's corps, occupying the city, outposts and all fortifications. The rest of 1st Army remained on the right riverbank, behind the Dnieper suburb; 2nd Army was about 8 *verstas* [5.3 miles] from Smolensk on the Dorogobuzh road. We faced two extreme prospects: either to accept a decisive battle or retreat. Because of the disadvantageous location, the former could not be attempted without exposing our armies to grave danger. The latter, meanwhile, was quite shameful. And so we decided to do both: to defend the city and to retreat.

Napoleon directed his first attack against the Malakhov gate. At 4 o'clock in the morning, a skirmish erupted there, lasting until

---

3 The Royal Bastion was a major earthwork constructed by the victorious Polish troops in 1611 during Polish King Sigismund III's invasion of Muscovy, and therefore bearing that appellation.

4 Radozhitskii refers to *khlebopeki*, i.e. soldiers assigned to baking duty.

noon as both sides gradually reinforced the combat. It seemed that Napoleon was waiting for us to make an attack against his right flank which he intentionally left exposed. He certainly wanted to lure our forces across the Dnieper so he could then deliver a decisive blow. However, seeing the cautious actions of [Barclay de Tolly] who limited himself to defending the city, [Napoleon] launched his main attack during the afternoon. A terrifying bombardment of the city's center and right flank had begun. Marshal Ney attacked on the [Russian] right while Davout approached the Mstislavlskii suburb. The terrain in Smolensk's vicinity, covered in brush and crisscrossed with ravines, proved to be very beneficial for enemy skirmishers. Standing on the right bank, we watched as they ran from one bush to another, letting out dreadful puffs of smoke [from their muskets.] The French soon approached the city along the Krasnyi road. The dreadful cannonade continued unabated. As we watched, our artillery fire destroyed caissons and spread disorder among the enemy columns while our skirmishers maintained a continuous fire against the French, who, however, continued their frenzied advance. Soon the enemy skirmishers appeared on the left side of the city, followed by [infantry] columns. A horse artillery company rushed ahead of them and, after unlimbering near the river, opened fire on the bridges to cut communications between the city and our [right] riverbank. A battery was deployed on our side at once to engage the enemy with equal determination. The artillery fire from both sides was murderous.

The battle reached its climax during the evening. The cumulative horrors of fighting turned indescribable! Hundreds of cannonballs and grenades whistled through the air and burst, one after another. The air above the city darkened from smoke, the earth groaned and it seemed that it disgorged hellish fires from deep inside – Death itself struggled to consume all of its victims. Reverberating noise, explosions, flames, smoke, groans and yells all combined into the dreadful chaos of a world on the verge of destruction.

THE RUSSIAN CAMPAIGN OF 1812

By 6 p.m., the French occupied all of the suburbs on the [left] side of the river. We only retained the Dnieper suburb on the right bank. The enemy shells ignited fires inside the city which embodied a new hellish vision for us: a battle in the midst of raging fire. Oh, what a firmness of soul Russians revealed as they defended a flaming Smolensk! Cannonballs, bullets, stone shards, falling burning timbers – everything threatened [Russian troops] with death and destruction. But following the examples of gallantry shown by General Dokhturov, Prince Eugene [of Württemberg[and Konovnitsyn, Russian soldiers remained firm. They chose to perish in the flames amidst the ruins, scorning all dangers. Russian soldiers did not betray the honor of their arms; they did not let the enemy inside the city until midnight, and only abandoned the city ruins in obedience to the will of their commander-in-chief.

At the same time, we also witnessed a moving scene. The unfortunate residents, our destitute compatriots, old men and women, with tears in their eyes, ran from the city toward the bridge, with forlorn cries, hands raised to the heavens and bitterly crying, "Oh Holy Mother, where are you! Oh, Miraculous Icon!" This icon of the Holy Mother of Smolensk had been evacuated from the city earlier on, and during the retreat to Moscow, it was carried amid the main artillery park, on a reserve artillery gun carriage belonging to Colonel Voyeikov's battery company. Many residents perished inside the city and on the bridge. They considered this adversity as the coming of Judgment Day and Napoleon as the Antichrist himself, leading the Devil's own host of demons.

As we stood on the bank of the Dnieper looking at the blazing city, an instinctive tremor of the heart revealed to us that we were still too weak to face our powerful enemy. At 9 p.m., the shooting subsided but Russian troops remained in the city.

During the battle at Smolensk our troops demonstrated examples of fierce resistance. Maybe they could have been able to stop the enemy's advance here if the fighting had continued because the

FROM SMOLENSK TO BORODINO

French failed to capture the city after a daylong battle. Rumors, which soon spread throughout the army, claimed that toward the end of this bloody battle, senior Russian generals begged the commander-in-chief [Barclay de Tolly] to delay the surrender of Smolensk for at least another day, pointing to the disordered state of the enemy and vouching for success through the resilience of Russian soldiers who were ready to die to the last in the ruins of Smolensk while annihilating the enemy and saving the Fatherland. But the commander-in-chief had reasons to act otherwise and so he ordered us to retreat.

At midnight General Dokhturov began moving the remnants of the brave troops who defended Smolensk across the bridge so that the French could not see them. General Korff and his cavalry were kept in the city to cover the retreat.

On 6 [18] August we frequently changed position on the road to Porechye as if in anticipation of a general battle. French columns briefly appeared on our side of the Dnieper but were driven back by General Konovnitsyn's division. We could see how the French triumphantly entered the ruins of the city we left behind: music and drums accompanied their parade. At that moment, the commander-in-chief rode up to an artillery officer, who stood with his cannon in front of the city, and told him, "Go ahead: congratulate them as well!" The officer aimed his guns at the house where we thought Napoleon had stopped and fired two explosive rounds at it. The fire continued to rage in the city and its glow, in the midst of an already gloomy day, cast a shade of grief on the faces of Russian soldiers.

The one-day battle of Smolensk was incomparably bloodier that the three-day battle near Vitebsk. Both sides fought hard, violently, and fearlessly. The glory of the battle belonged to General Dokhturov, who with 30,000 Russians held out against 72,000 besieging French.

During the night of 7 [19] August the 1st Army moved from Smolensk in two columns: the left, consisting of the 5th and 6th Infantry Corps and two cavalry corps, moved on a safer road through the village of Prudische while the right, consisting of the

2nd, 3rd and 4th Corps with a rearguard under General Korff, was ordered to proceed across a hilly countryside, following the road through Krakhotkino and Zhabino to Bredikhino in order to get to the main [Moscow] road, which was protected by General Tuchkov III's detachment in front of the village of Lubino.

At 9 p.m. on 6 [18] August my unit set off with the right column from Smolensk, marching through the night of 7 [19] August across hills and ravines covered with dense shrubs. The night was dark and damp. At dawn, sleep overcame me so I sat on a gun carriage and, leaning my head against the carriage, gave myself away to sweet dreams. Just as my cannon descended on a slope, English Lord Wilson[5] happened to be passing by. The gunners were holding on to me so I did not fall off the carriage, and, upon seeing a senior officer, they began to wake me up. Seeing what was going on, the venerable lord was much taken by their care for their officer, and gestured to them to let me sleep. When I woke, they told me about the considerate "red" general who, as I learned later, was an Englishman assigned to our Commander-in-Chief and tasked by the [British] envoy to serve as an observer [to the Russian army].

At dawn on 7 [19] August we approached the main road, where General Tuchkov's detachment waited for us, and heard a cannonade coming from behind us. It was Prince of Wurttemberg's division from the 2nd Corps, engaging the French at the village of Gorbunovo, which the French had captured, thereby cutting off the rearguard of General Korff. The French then turned to the main road and advanced toward General Tuchkov's detachment, which held positions between the villages of Toporovshina and Latynina on the Stragan Rivulet. The enemy engaged this detachment before the 2nd Corps, which was delayed at Gorbunovo, managed to get to the main road. Meanwhile we were moving with the 4th Corps, ahead of the 2nd Corps, and had already passed the village of

---

5 Sir Robert Wilson, British commissioner to the Russian army. Wilson did not have a title.

Lubino when we were turned back to reinforce General Tuchkov's detachment, which the French engaged so vigorously that it was forced to retreat across the Stragan Rivulet.

By 3 o'clock in the afternoon the battle intensified. A ferocious firefight was being waged in the brush all along the line. Because of the smoke that rose incessantly from musket fire, the brush seemed to be on fire. For several hours the French had tried in vain to break through our center. A murderous rain of lead claimed many victims. Skirmishers could hardly see each other, and death stealthily claimed the brave souls. The attacking enemy columns were annihilated by the canister rounds fired by our batteries as well as the bayonets of our grenadiers. Meanwhile, the French [VIII] Corps of General Junot, accompanied by numerous cavalry, appeared on the hill against our left flank. Our 4th Corps was immediately moved to face this new threat.

Staff-Captain Figner, as the commander of 3rd Light Artillery Company, was still in reserve when the regiments of our corps moved left and up the hill. However, he understood that we would be soon committed to the battle and ordered the available wine rations to be given to his artillery crews. He borrowed this method of maintaining soldiers' courage from the French, who, upon falling into our hands, usually carried rum or vodka instead of water, in the canister behind their knapsacks... After wishing his gun crews success in victory, Figner went ahead, out of ordinary curiosity, to observe the battle, but soon returned and ordered everyone to mount the gun carriages and caissons at once. We quickly rode to the left flank but had to pass through swamp that delayed our movement. Having moved through the marsh, our guns began to ascend a steep hill, where a cavalry melee was taking place. We could hear a rumbling noise, shouting and occasional cannon fire. Suddenly to the left of us, the Cossacks descended the hill; some of them quickly turned back but three Cossacks kept descending, accompanying a fat Württemberg trumpeter who was unhorsed. He wore a blue uniform with red lapels and big boots, which occasionally tripped him. The poor lad had probably blown his trumpet too much since he was bathed in sweat and red-faced as usually happens after a lot of work. But he seemed to be proud of the fact that three Cossacks were assigned to escort him.

Climbing up the hill, we observed a rather curious spectacle. The Pernovskii Regiment stood in line on the top of hill, with six of our cannon on its right flank while the remaining guns had to remain on the slope because of a lack of space. In front of the Pernovskii Regiment, we could see blue, red, gray and green hussars deployed, by squadrons and with horse artillery guns, in the brush. The cavalry melee unfolded before our eyes. It was fascinating to see how a few squadrons of French hussars charged at our horsemen, who fled at full gallop before receiving reinforcements, turned around and drove the French back. Only shrapnel and bullets stopped their charges but as they recalled, they were again attacked and pursued by the French. Such fighting resembled the knightly tournaments: some cavalrymen fell from their horses; some, finding themselves amidst the enemy, were waving their sabers; one shot his pistol, the other hacked [with his saber] at the enemy; horses crashed into each other, became frenzied and rushed away... To the right of the hill Prince Gurielov was with the Polotskii Infantry Regiment, deployed in woods that covered the hill slopes. At one point he moved forward from the woods to attack the enemy cavalry's's flank, but quickly faced a similar threat and was forced to stop.

Figner's cannon remained idle because they had to shoot through our own men. Meanwhile, as I observed the overall course of the battle, I noticed French infantry on our right flank, moving through the brush at the bottom of the hill. The French drove our jagers back. I rushed to inform Figner about this, emphasizing the consequences if the French managed to get behind us. He told me to take six guns, descend from the hill and move to the main road while he followed me with the remaining guns. I was delayed by the swamp at the bottom of the hill and only managed to move five guns before the sixth got stuck in the swamp. As they came out of the brush, the [French] skirmishers stumbled directly upon my guns. Upon seeing my cannon so close to them, the French rushed toward me. Their bullets began to buzz sharply above us, and the tight space and difficult terrain prevented me from deploying for action, so I decided to hasten toward the main road. The crackling of musket fire and clouds of smoke kept approaching us; bullets began to pierce our gunners, horses, some struck gun carriages.... Our jagers, carrying their muskets at the trail and crouching low as they did so, hurried to hide from the deadly lead behind my guns. Their officer shouted to them, "Where are you going, lads? Come back, please, you should be ashamed!" But nobody listened to him. Suddenly generals – Commander-in-Chief Barclay de Tolly, accompanied by Lord [Robert] Wilson, Count [Alexander] Kutaisov, Osterman, Orlov, Korff and others – appeared in front of us. They all shouted at the fleeing men, "Where are you going! Stop! Turn back!" The soldiers stopped and turned back. The Commander-in-Chief rode up to me and asked sternly, "Where did you come from?" - "From there" I replied, pointing to the hill on the left. And he went onwards. The generals were followed by dense columns of grenadiers from Count Arakcheyev's Leib-Grenadier and Yekaterinoslavskiii Grenadier Regiments: these were tall fellows with pale faces, holding their muskets at the ready and marching at a brisk pace to meet death. With the cry of "Hurrah!" they charged into the brush and restored order with bayonets. Five minutes later, many of them, bloodied and half dead, returned leaning on the shoulders of their comrades ... It was impossible not to shudder as one witnessed the withering of the finest colors of the Russian might.

 The fast approaching darkness failed to end the ferocious battle. Despite our persistence, the French continued to fight until midnight ignoring the heavy casualties they suffered. They lost a general of division [Charles Etienne Gudin] who was killed, but in return captured General [Pavel] Tuchkov,[6] it being this which had caused our skirmishers to flee. General Konovnitsyn and his grenadiers, however, had managed to save the day and hold the position.

After my departure, Staff Captain Figner remained behind with six guns, with the Pernovskii Regiment on the left flank. His personal courage saved my cannon which had been mired in the swamp. We witnessed his gallantry. Upon observing from the hill top that the French had driven our skirmishers out of the brush and could capture the mired gun, he descended from the hill with a saber and pistol in hand. His commanding voice rallied the fleeing soldiers. Figner managed to gather about fifteen men whom he hid in the woods. As the throng of Frenchmen, shouting incessantly "En avant! En avant!", approached the ambush, Figner ordered his men to fire a volley and then rushed with a naked saber and pistol toward the officer who led the French, grabbed him and threatened to kill him [if he did not surrender]. This surprise attack completely stopped the French – the officer surrendered while his men showed their backs to us. As Figner dragged the officer, a chevalier of the Legion of Honour, by the collar, he came across the Commander-in-Chief who, having learned of Figner's feat, immediately congratulated him with a promotion to captain. We were all thrilled by the feat and congratulated Figner. He unexpectedly became unusually contemplative and withdrawn and did not want to do anything in the company, leaving it to me as the next senior officer.

This combat had a great effect on me. So much had the constant fire, the fleeing skirmishers and the proximity of danger frightened me that I kept hearing gunfire throughout the night even though there was none, while I could not get the vision of the scrawny and power-

---

6 General Pavel Tuchkov commanded a brigade in the 17th Division of the 2nd Corps and was tasked with defending a road junction at Lubino/Valutina Gora. During the battle, he led a counterattack with the Ekaterinoslavskii Grenadier Regiment but was captured after receiving a bayonet wound to the abdomen and several saber cuts to the head. He was well treated by Marshal Alexander Berthier and eventually met Napoleon, who had him transported to Metz, where Tuchkov remained until early 1814.

blackened visions of the French skirmishers who had pursued our jagers out of my mind. Between them, continued exposure to the horrors of war and my recent fever had affected my mind. Besides, having marched for over thirty *verstas* [20 miles] on very poor roads in darkness since yesterday evening, we had spent the entire day on our feet and in the midst of battle, only to continue retreating throughout the night. I was not the only one exhausted by such exertion, and both men and horses barely trudged along.

After the battle, we stopped for about two hours at our main headquarters, crossed the Brovenka River at night and joined the rest of the army at Lubino before resuming our retreat. On 8 [20] August, we crossed the Dnieper at the Solovyevo crossing. This location was very important to us, and, if they had anticipated our move, the French could have caused us plenty of harm. The riverbanks here are low lying, sandy and covered on both sides with small woods that are quite disadvantageous for defending against an enemy. We stopped for the night four *verstas* [2.5 miles] from the crossing.

From there on, the French pursuit eased off as the most recent fights had cooled their ardor. Besides, it was said that Napoleon was still at Smolensk, pondering [what to do next.]

At dawn of the following day, 1st Army's entire artillery concentrated into a general park before moving to the Moscow River. We marched by companies where possible and kept passing each other by as we moved. The dust and heat were intolerable. The guns moved six abreast on the wide road, which was so ploughed up [by carriages] that in some places we walked knee-deep in finely ground dirt that felt like powder; while the wheels rolled without making any noise. The entire artillery park was commanded by Colonel Voyeikov. For several *verstas* back and forth, one could not see anything but artillery and baggage trains moving in dense clouds of dust that kept rising to the sky. We walked as if shrouded in fog; the sun seemed purple and neither the greenery by the side of the road nor the paint on gun carriages could be discerned. Soldiers were covered from head to toe in gray dust, and our faces and hands were black from dust and sweat. We swallowed and breathed the dust. For all that the heat tormented us with thirst, we could not find any refreshments. In these miserable conditions, we happened to pass by a crowd of French prisoners who had been captured in the last battle and were happy to see us hastily retreating. They mockingly told us that we would not get away from Napoleon because they now made up the vanguard of his army.

I must admit that our soldiers became very disheartened after the battle at Smolensk. The blood that had been shed in the ruins of Smolensk and all the effort made to resist the enemy, not to mention the fact that we were now retreating along the Moscow road into the depths of Russia itself, had made each and every one of us feel powerless against our terrible conqueror. Each of us witnessed heartrending visions of the perishing Fatherland. Residents from nearby settlements ran to us, leaving the greater part of their positions to their friends and enemies. To the rear and, indeed, all round us, burning villages announced the approaching French troops. The Cossacks destroyed everything that was left behind following the passage of our troops so that the enemy found only barren and desolate land everywhere. Thus, desperate Russia tormented her own womb.

After marching for 26 *verstas* [17 miles], we bivouacked at the village of Usvyat, about eight *verstas* [5.5 miles] from Dorogobuzh. The following day, the artillery was again distributed between regiments. Moving from one place to another, troops changed positions twice that day. By evening we barely managed to settle down at a position that also proved to be disadvantageous. We remained there only till the following morning.

On 11 [23] August, the enemy attacked our rearguard, causing alarm throughout the entire army. We were moved to the other side of the main road, closer to the town, where the army established a new position until nightfall, while the rearguard kept fighting. At midnight of 12 [24] August, we ignited large bonfires at our camp before marching for seven *verstas* [5 miles] to Dorogobuzh. There, the Commander-in-Chief [Barclay de Tolly] seemed to intend to give the French another battle because the army was deployed in a strong position and entrenchments thrown up around the artillery batteries. Our artillery company was assigned a spot on the extreme right flank, in the gardens of the suburbs. The town [Dorogobuzh], located on a hill, remained behind us.

The Cossacks of the unforgettable Matvei Ivanovich [Platov] distinguished themselves in the rearguard. They were continually engaged in fighting with enemy cavalry and, as they used to say, carried the French on their own shoulders. On the road, we encountered a few Cossacks accompanying comrades who had been wounded fighting with the rearguard, and engaged them in a conversation. They complained that even they could no longer resist the enemy force; that today, the 12th [24] August, they were engaged in such a fierce fight with the French that they could not recognize each other in the thick dust that surrounded them. The result – at least so said one Cossack – was that we lost some three hundred men. "We can no longer endure this," he continued. "The accursed [French] keep snapping at our heels. And don't let me get started about their cannon: just as we charge their hussars, their cursed guns begin firing fire-crackers [shells] and pellets [canister] at us... In truth, even Matvei Ivanovich would refuse to fight here; so you get on with it all on your own." Indeed, a few days later we heard that Ataman Platov had become ill and left the army. Such news was unpleasant. As we marched, the soldiers walked with their heads downcast; strict discipline was no longer upheld. Each soldier walked they way he wanted, preoccupied by the thought of what would happen next? Our officers, gathering in small groups, talked about the impending downfall of the Fatherland and wondered about their own fate. The arms, which we carried so eagerly to defend the Fatherland, now seemed useless and burdensome. Dust and heat exhausted many soldiers and made them leave the road and seek merriment on the side.

We did not remain at the strong position at Dorogobuzh for long. Upon learning that the enemy's main force sought to march upstream on the Dnieper to bypass us at Vyazma, we broke our camps during the night of 12 [24] August and resumed our withdrawal. The rearguard set the bridges on fires and the flames soon reached the town as well. Concerned that we would be cut off, we kept marching throughout the 13th, covering some 60 *verstas* [40 miles] to Vyazma.

As my company reached Vyazma, I decided to travel into town, out of curiosity, hoping to find the cookies that made Vyazma so famous. I found the town very decent, with plenty of stone houses, churches, and shops, but it was largely deserted. Some of the residents who had failed to get out of town were running in utter confusion through the streets, while others were loading carts with belongings taken out of their houses. The shops were still open, and although goods had been removed, there was still enough left for the soldiers who, on the pretext of fatigue or thirst, entered the houses and plundered. Finding no cookies, I took in this display of futile avarice and, shaking my head, returned full of sorrow to the campsite.

During the night of 15 [27] August we left our camp and, passing through town, took a new position behind it at around 10 a.m. Marching at night was easier and cooler; besides, the darkness of night concealed gloomy faces, while the drowsiness we felt during the day caused us to ignore the anguish of what was happening around us. The following day we just marched for 10 *verstas* [7 miles], to the village of Federovskoe. The rearguard took a strong position in front of Vyazma but somebody had rashly set fire to the bridges and the flames soon spread to the town, causing the rearguard to ford the river and deploy behind the town.

The flat plains between Vyazma and Tsarevo-Zaimishche greatly facilitated cavalry movement, so diverse and numerous [Russian] and enemy cavalry, accompanied by horse artillery batteries, converged onto these plains. Positioning themselves in full view of one another, they maneuvered back and forth, while the flankers amused themselves skirmishing. The French did not seek to engage us because our entire army was nearby and ready to support the rearguard. Besides, although the French columns advanced on both sides of the road, they were desperate for supplies since they found nothing but utter devastation in our wake. The war had transcended the limits of humanity, becoming more uncontrolled, implacable, and destructive. It had to end in the destruction of one of the two warring powers. The French, still inspired and enjoying numerical superiority, expected a glorious end to this campaign, while, after losing several provinces and half of our men, and failing to stop the enemy either at Vitebsk or Smolensk, we had been thrown into profound depression and thought of nothing but the disastrous fate of our Fatherland. Having troops, we still seemed powerless; having arms, we still appeared unarmed. And so, thousands of courageous but distracted and disheartened warriors marched onwards. The present disasters of their Fatherland plunged Russians into an understandable blindness. Who could have expected a happy ending after these events? We were all eager for a decisive battle as the sole consolation for our misery, as the only means of redeeming the dying Fatherland, or finding death in its ruin.

The troops were in this [depressed] state of mind when news of the arrival of a new Commander-in-Chief, Prince Kutuzov, spread like an electric charge [*elektricheski*] throughout the army. The moment of joy was indescribable: the very name of this commander revived everyone's spirit, from rank-and-file to generals. Everyone who could rushed to greet the venerable leader and to get inspired by his aspirations to save Russia. Officers cheerfully congratulated each other with this fortunate change of circumstances; upon hearing about the arrival of their beloved commander, the soldiers, who usually walked slowly and lazily when they went to fetch water with their kettles, ran to the river shouting "Hurrah," as if already imagining that they were driving the enemy back. An expression quickly spread among the soldiers: "Kutuzov has finally come to beat the French!" Veteran soldiers recalled their campaigns under Kutuzov during the reign of

THE RUSSIAN CAMPAIGN OF 1812

[Empress] Catherine, recounted his exploits from past campaigns, especially during the battle at Krems [Durrenstein in 1805] and the most recent destruction of the Turkish army [at Ruse] on the Danube [in 1811].

For many, these were fresh memories. They remembered Kutuzov's miraculous survival after a musket bullet pierced both of his temples. It was said that Napoleon had long called him an "Old Fox" and that [Generalissimo Alexander] Suvorov used to say that "even Ribas[7] could not deceive Kutuzov." Such tales, flying from mouth to mouth, only further increased the army's confidence in their new commander, who had a Russian name, mind and heart, hailed from a famous family and was well-known for his exploits. In short, Prince Kutuzov's arrival at this most critical moment for Russia, when Providence cast a dark veil of demise on her, had clearly revealed how the presence of a beloved military leader could resurrect the spirit of a disheartened army and society. Had not the ever-memorable Suvorov, with a mere handful of Russian warriors, demonstrated that soldiers' love for their leader was not just a dream but a tangible thing capable of producing miracles?

Upon joining the army, Prince Kutuzov immediately knew what the Russian army had been impatiently waiting for. He understood that, to quench their thirst for vengeance, he had to give them a decisive battle. But the plains at Vyazma did not present suitably advantageous positions to deploy the entire army, so Kutuzov decided to retreat even further, despite having already assumed the appearance of the formidable defender of Russia. Napoleon was informed about the new Commander-in-Chief in Vyazma. Recalling Kutuzov's reputation as the "Old Fox", he checked his continued offensive in favour of what

---

[7] Joseph Ribas y Boyons (1749-1800) was born into a Spanish noble family, served in Naples and entered Russian service in 1774. He quickly advanced through ranks, becoming a rear admiral in 1791 and admiral in 1799. He was famous for his shrewd and devious character.

looked like taking various precautions against a surprise attack, and this allowed us to have a day of rest on 18 [30] August.

On 20 [1] September, we marched five *verstas* [3.3 miles] beyond the town of Gzhatsk and occupied positions around the village of Durykino. The quartermasters, including myself, began assigning spots in anticipation of a decisive battle. We learned that, having taken Gzhatsk, Napoleon halted his troops in order to rest them and prepare for the battle which he expected to be offered by Prince Kutuzov. We were also pleased to hear news about the arrival of Suvorov's contemporary, the Russian noble, General Miloradovich, who brought 15,000 inexperienced troops with him. Everything gradually changed for the better, proper order was restored, and equipment was refurbished. We could at last once more hear songs and music in the camp, which had not happened for a while. Despite the fact that we continued retreating, so profoundly had Prince Kutuzov's presence revived the spirit of the entire army, we now expected that we would soon be advancing to fight the French.

Chapter V

From Borodino to Moscow

On 22 August [3 September], our troops passed through the village of Borodino and took up a position chosen by our new commander-in-chief some eight *verstas* [5.3 miles] from Mozhaisk. It was here that we first saw the *opolchenye*: Russian peasants armed with pikes and muskets which they barely knew how to hold.

The following day was a day of rest, so Figner and I decided to observe our troops' deployment. It was impossible to find a better position in the vicinity. The Kolocha River flowed in front of the position, from a large forest on the left, and, after making a turn around the right flank, merged with the Moscow River [to the north]. The hills on the right bank were quite steep and overlooked the left. The main road from Smolensk to Moscow ran across the Kolocha River and through the village of Borodino, almost in the center of our position. The high mound there seemed to have been deliberately designed to observe the entire battlefield. From there a chain of hills extended to the left flank, ending at the edge of a vast forest that covered our entire left flank and rear. The Russian army and its reserves were deployed in three lines in the area between the forest [on the left] and the mouth of the Kolocha River [on the right], which is about seven *verstas* [5 miles] wide. Along the entire front, entrenchments had been thrown up on the heights to protect the artillery. The newly arrived *opolchenye* dug them by day and by night. As we moved along the line, Figner noticed a weakness on our left flank, despite the redoubt that seemingly protected it. He recalled that in previous campaigns we had lost battles because of a weakness on our left flank, which Napoleon constantly targeted. He predicted that the same would happen here as well. "Mark my words," he told me, "Napoleon will direct all his forces against this [left] flank and push us into the Moscow River." Indeed, a more careful observation of the position revealed that even though our position seemed strong, the old Smolensk road to Mozhaisk, which ran through the forest on the left flank and into our rear, remained undefended while the right flank was anchored on the village of Maslovo, far removed from the center of our position. Marching from the village of Valuevo toward our center at Borodino, the enemy could exploit the local terrain by deploying all his forces against our left flank and crushing its center by taking the Old Smolensk road. In effect, the enemy could confine our army to a narrow angle between the mouth of the Kolocha River and the Moscow River. However, as events later revealed, facing the Russian army at last, Napoleon was only interested in winning a quick victory, and therefore did not concern himself with strategic intricacies, instead preferring to crush us by means of a straight-forward head-on attack. Prince Kutuzov soon perceived the importance of defending the old Smolensk road, and, on the day of battle, deployed General Tuchkov's corps there with the support of some jagers and the Moscow *opolchenye*.

On 24 August [5 September] the French, marching from the village of Gridnevo, attacked our rearguard under the command of General Konovnitsyn, which was deployed in front of the Kolotsk Monastery. The enemy closely pursued it all the way to Borodino. We could hear the approaching cannonade from early morning onwards. Finally, in the afternoon, Napoleon had the pleasure of observing our entire army standing firm in a menacing manner and ready to engage his troops in a decisive battle. Noticing an isolated redoubt on our left flank, which had been placed in a forward position to draw him in, he immediately issued orders to capture it. By evening the redoubt was in the hands of the French, though they suffered heavy casualties in the process. With that out of the way, Napoleon began to deploy his army, choosing the captured redoubt as the center of his offensive movement.

The following day, both warring armies stood in sight of each other, surrounded by a mysterious silence that usually precedes a frightful tempest. Both commanders were preoccupied issuing orders for the upcoming battle. Captain Figner's light artillery company was scattered in the brushwood opposite the village of Novoe Seltso, which was intentionally burnt down the previous night so it would not serve as cover for the enemy. Enjoying some free time, Figner invited Lieutenant Nagel and me to visit the skirmisher chain and observe the enemy camp.

We forded the Kolocha River near the ruins of the burnt out village. We observed a cavalry chain of French dragoons in an open field a half a *versta* ahead of us, followed by a squad of dismounted troopers standing at an outpost. Next to us was the village of Loginovo, where numerous cavalrymen were busy gathering large bundles of straw that were then dragged to their bivouacs. We approached to within musket range of the [enemy] outposts so we could see the courageous faces of the dragoons underneath their massive *sisaks* [helmets]. They were covered with lightly colored coats and sat on horses so steadfastly that they seemed to be dug into the ground. Beyond the chain we could see troops moving from one place to another. Having seen as much as we desired, we returned safely to our guns without suffering any misfortune for our insolence.

In the evening, all regiments held services praying for victory for the Orthodox Russian host in the upcoming battle. An order soon came from the Commander-in-Chief [Kutuzov] which, among other things, required all branches to support each other during the battle so that cavalry assisted the infantry and infantry helped the artillery; that the injured men should not be accompanied by several healthy soldiers, which would open gaps in our ranks; that the reserves

FROM BORODINO TO MOSCOW

should be committed only on his orders and, most importantly, to avoid unnecessary shooting [so as not to waste ammunition.] It was said that Prince Kutuzov, while riding through the ranks and seeing cheerfulness on the faces of Russian soldiers who were eager to die to the last for the Fatherland, told his companions, "The French will break their teeth on us, but that is a pity since, having shattered them, we would have nothing left to smash."

The Russians did not have sufficient forces. We had up to 115,000 regular troops, 7,000 Cossacks, 10,000 *opolchenye* and 640 guns. The French had 190,000 of their best troops and up to 1,000 guns. However, our disparity in numbers was evened out by our love for the Fatherland and a thirst for vengeance. Remembering the former glory of victorious Russians arms, each soldier burned with impatience to engage the enemy so their blood could wash away the humiliation that all of us had suffered. We were all confident of the leadership of our wise commander, for he was a veteran of the field of battle.

The French had also prepared for battle, but, rather than love of their Fatherland, they were sustained by no more than their ravenous desire for plunder and the glory of conquest. They had gone too far [into Russia] and sought victory both to save themselves and to preserve the honor of their arms. For the last two and a half months they had eagerly sought a decisive battle that would accomplish their goals. The French had suffered great hardships, experiencing hitherto unheard of deprivation. They therefore faced two outcomes: if defeated, they faced inevitable destruction; if they emerged victorious, pleasant prospects flattered their ambition: thus, Moscow lay open before them beyond the battlefield, while it seemed that they would only have to march over the corpses of the sons of Russia to reach their spoils, enjoy sensual pleasures, gain a glorious peace and finally return to their Fatherland. In short, the fate of Napoleon's Grande Armée would be decided on the field of Borodino. The Grande Armée was supported by almost all of Europe, with the French, Germans, Italians, Spaniards, Poles and others ready to follow the

THE RUSSIAN CAMPAIGN OF 1812

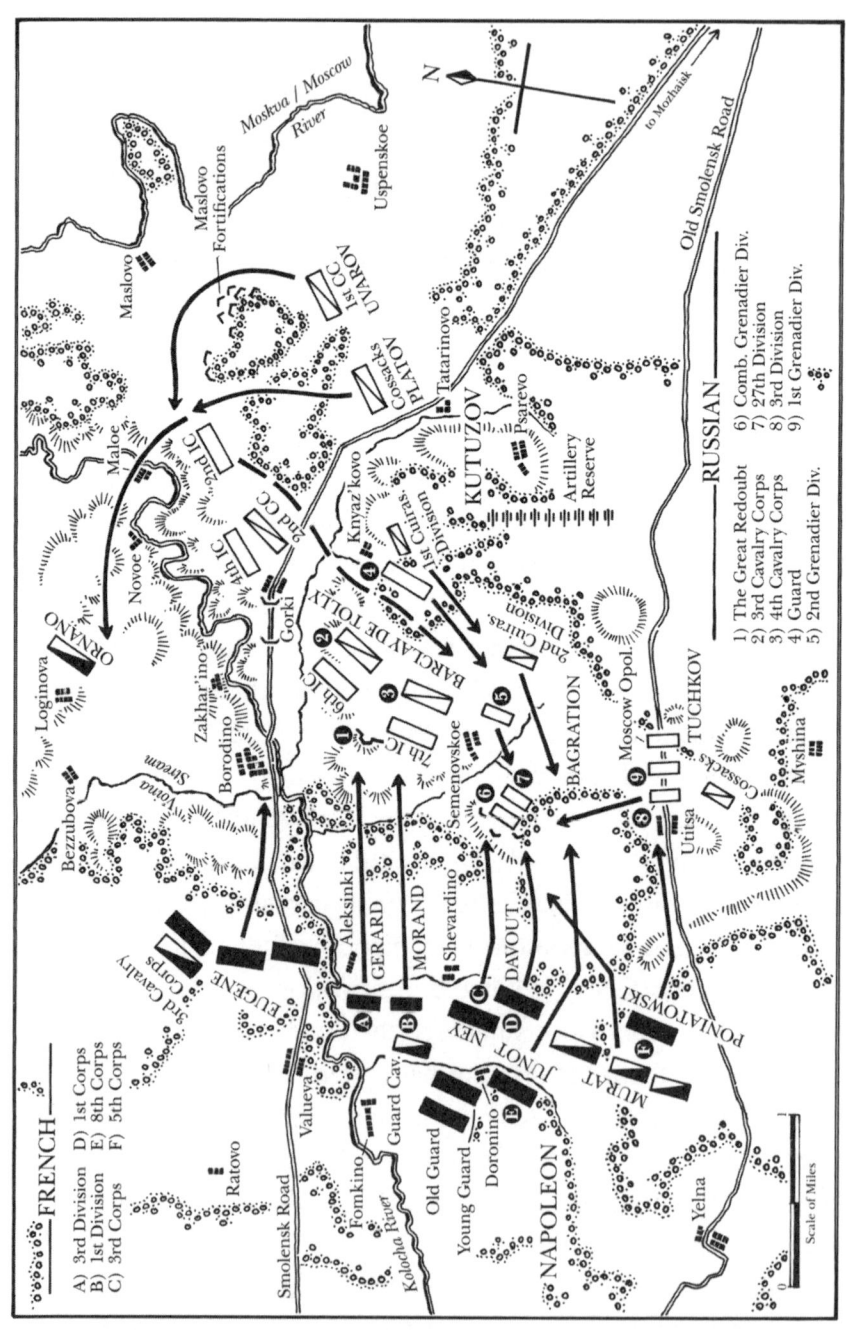

The Battle of Borodino.

slightest whim of that extraordinary man, and either win or die. And die they did, together with the glory of their all-conquering genius.[1]

The day of preparation for the terrible battle seemed fleeting. The complete silence that reigned in both armies was a harbinger of impending horrors. How many thousands of future victims of human enmity still enjoyed life that day only to turn to dust the next! How many brave and ambitious men were preparing to distinguish themselves, not thinking about death, only to enter into the eternity of oblivion the following day! Thus, a man is destined to remain the plaything of passions: to reach for the heavens with his mind and to disappear in earthly irrelevance.

The sun shone brightly and glided its golden rays over the fatal steel of our bayonets and muskets. It sparkled with brilliant light on the bronze of our guns. Everything was getting ready for bloodshed on the morrow. The Moscow militiamen were completing earthworks for the battery, artillery was deployed and ammunition distributed. Soldiers cleaned and sharpened bayonets, cleaned sword-belts and shoulder-belts. In short, 300,000 men from both armies were preparing for the great, terrible day.

As the night approached, the bivouacs of the warring forces flared with numerous fires all around. The fires turned the dark clouds in the sky into a crimson twilight and the flames in the sky only foretold of bloodshed on the ground. The forces gathered here were vast indeed and the impending carnage promised to enter the annals of history.

The Battle of Borodino has been described by numerous witnesses and is known to almost everyone. Therefore, avoiding unnecessary repetition, I will describe only some incidents from this battle.

---

[1] For the invasion of Russia, Napoleon undertook massive military preparations. Despite having over quarter million troops tied down in Spain, the French emperor drew upon the resources of his vast empire and raised some 600,000 men for a new war in the east. Of these, just half were French; the rest were Poles, Italians, Swiss, Bavarians, Badenese, Württembergians, Hessians, Westphalians, Saxons, Croats, Danes, Spaniards, and Portuguese, supported by two large contingents of Austrians and Prussians.

THE RUSSIAN CAMPAIGN OF 1812

As the sun rose at dawn, numerous guns, howitzers, and licornes[2] erupted into a ferocious cannonade all along the line between the left flank and the center. The cannon fire was so frequent that there were no lulls in the explosions that, thunder-like, continued incessantly, producing a man-made earthquake. Thick clouds of smoke, curling around the batteries, ascended to heaven and soon obscured the sun, which became veiled in a bloody shroud as if affected by human rage and ferocity. Standing on the right flank, Figner and I long remained quiet spectators of this spectacle and stood silently next to our guns, expecting orders to join the battle at any moment. The enemy cannonballs reached us in leaps and bounds or rolling on the ground; shells exploded in the air scattering numerous splinters, while making a terrifying noise.

Meanwhile, a fierce battle was, underway on the left flank. The Russians courageously held their ground in their redoubts while the French paid a heavy price in casualties for every step they made [toward the Russian positions.] One could not but wonder at their boldness and audacity as they pushed onward to their death. One could not but wonder at the composure of the Russians who held their ground and repulsed assaults by superior enemy forces.

After the French captured the [Great Redoubt in the] middle of our line for the first time and were then driven back, the infantry of the 4th Corps was ordered to move forward to reinforce those fighting around the lunette [the Great Redoubt]. The stories of our exploits quickly spread through the ranks. Carried away by martial excitement, Major T. of the Yeletskii Regiment galloped along our line proclaiming that the French had been defeated and the King of Naples himself

---

2 Licorne (*edinorog* in Russian) was the French name of a Russian muzzle-loading howitzer devised in 1757 by M. Danilov and S. Martynov and adopted by artillery commander General Peter Shuvalov. The licorne represented a hybrid between the howitzers and conventional cannon, with a longer barrel than contemporary howitzers, giving projectiles a flatter trajectory, but longer range. Its unusual name comes from unicorn-shaped handles on the barrel of the guns, an homage to Shuvalov's whose family coat of arms featured this mythic beast.

captured. This major had a slight speech defect, so he made us laugh as he yelled as loud as he could "Lads [*biyatsy*]! Muyat [sic!] is captured!" This false Murat turned out to be General Bonnamy, who, as a Russian grenadier was about to bayonet him, decided to save himself by shouting "I am the King!" So the moustached grenadier grabbed him by the scruff of the neck and dragged him away to the Commander-in-Chief. Prince Kutuzov immediately congratulated the grenadier with a promotion to the rank of non-commissioned officer and granted him the badge of distinction of the Military Order of St. George. However, this encounter near the lunette cost us dearly as well: it was there that Count Kutaisov, our artillery commander and a man whose personal qualities pointed to a bright future, was killed.

The 4th Corps infantry moved to the center, while the artillery remained stationary in reserve [in its original location]. Figner and I eagerly waited to join in this bloody carnage. Figner was so impatient that he repeatedly went to General Miloradovich, who then commanded our right flank and begged him to assign his company a spot in the front line. But there was still no need for us, and so we waited in vain until noon. [At last] we were ordered to move our cannon out of the brush, deploy them in line and remain ready for battle. Out of curiosity, I climbed the nearest hill. Located in front of the village of Gorki, this was occupied by a Russian battery that was repeatedly firing at the enemy columns. From its top I could observe a vast battlefield that lay open in front of me. I saw our infantry, deployed in dense masses, clashing with the enemy. I observed how [infantry units] approached one another, fired battalion volleys, redeployed, scattered and finally disappeared altogether. Only dead remained behind while the wounded returned back. They were followed by other columns that clashed and disappeared in the same manner. The sight of human slaughter astounded me so much that I could no longer look at it, and, with my heart aching deeply, I returned back to my cannon. The French cuirassiers and lancers then charged at the infantry of the 4th Corps but were driven back by our musket fire. The 34th Jager and Pernovskii [Infantry] Regiments distinguished themselves particularly on this occasion. The latter regiment, led by the gallant General Choglokov, deployed in a battalion square and charged enemy cavalry. The grenadiers in the front ranks even pursued the French with their bayonets. The hussars and uhlans deployed in support of this regiment pursued the French cavalry all the way to where the enemy infantry was positioned.

It seemed that the Commander-in-Chief still entertained hopes for victory as long as the large lunette in the center of our line, and the village of Semeyonovskoe on our left hand, remained in our possession. While dealing with the danger threatening our left flank, he sought to recover our lost positions by committing all his forces to turn the tide of battle in favor of the Russian arms. To divert the enemy's attention, he ordered Lieutenant General Uvarov, with the 1st Cavalry Corps, to cross the Kolocha River and attack the enemy left flank that lay exposed beyond the village of Borodino. We watched with pleasure as our cavalry, red and blue hussars and uhlans, moving in long lines on the other side of the river, charged at the French cavalry and drove it far beyond Borodino. It then attacked the enemy batteries. The Elizavetgradskii Hussar Regiment even captured two cannon. But the enemy's four infantry regiments, deployed in squares near Borodino, advanced against our cavalry, which attacked each of them alternately and, unable to break any of them, was forced to retreat. At that moment, Figner received the order to move his artillery to the village of Gorki. As we moved, we heard intense musket fire as the French targeted our cavalry and then suddenly a few scattered hussars galloped past us. Some of them, already wounded, fell from their horses in front us – among them was one handsome officer, who was pierced by a bullet in the chest and brought down just two paces in front of us… We soon saw two Don-Cossack regiments skillfully deploy in open order without any casualties despite artillery fire, then regroup and charge the French.

FROM BORODINO TO MOSCOW

By noon, when the Viceroy of Italy launched the last assault against our redoubt on the knoll [*kurgannyi lunette*], the musket and gun fire that both sides directed at this location turned this hill into a fire breathing mound. Furthermore, all the glittering sabers, broadswords, bayonets, helmets and armor, under the bright rays of the setting sun, presented a terrible but majestic view. Standing at the village of Gorki, we were also witnesses to this bloody assault. Our cavalry mingled with the enemy in a fierce melee. In every direction men shot and sabers stabbed each other. The French finally reached the lunette and our cannon, after a final volley, fell silent. A muffled cry announced that the enemy had indeed broken inside the ramparts and hand-to-hand combat with bayonets ensued. French General Caulaincourt was the first to storm the redoubt from the rear, and the first to be killed. Attacked by our infantrymen beyond the ditch, his cuirassiers faced a hail of bullets and were driven back with great loss. Meanwhile, the enemy infantry kept climbing onto the redoubt from every direction. Although driven back by Russian bayonets defending the ditches filled with corpses, their fresh columns furiously pushed forward to die, replacing those that were broken. Our men met them with equal fury, dying together with their enemies. At last, the French charged wrathfully into the redoubt [sic!] and killed everyone they encountered, especially the artillerists who had maintained a deadly fire from their battery. Thus, for all that this was the last success achieved by their forces, the knoll fell into enemy hands. Piles of corpses lay inside and outside the ramparts. Almost all of the brave men who defended it perished in the process. So ferocious was this combat.

We still retained one larger redoubt which maintained a persistent cannonade against Borodino. But, as the French were already depleted by their heavy losses and Napoleon only had the Guard in reserve, the enemy did not undertake a new attack on this last redoubt, instead limiting his actions to artillery fire. The enemy also sought shelter from the murderous fire of our batteries. The artillery fire continued on both sides until evening when it began to subside, initially on the enemy side. This was contrary to their custom since the French had a habit of intensifying their fire and attacks in all directions during the evening as a [tangible] indication of their victory. But this time they were even forced to admit their impotence. Finally, their artillery fell silent, followed by our cannon. In this fashion this dreadful battle slowly ended.

The crimson sun, having dipped its last ray of light in the blood of so many dead, disappeared over the horizon as if shuddering from the terrible slaughter that unfolded beneath it. Darkness descended on the field of death, and the gunpowder smoke and stench enveloped the vast battlefield in a heavy mist.

Thus ended the famous battle of 26 August [7 September]. The enemy captured all the redoubts on the left flank and on the left side of the main road. But they only dislodged us from our position on one flank, where they occupied one third of the position. Thus, they could claim no more than a half-victory. Their's was not a complete victory – the Russians were not broken or disordered and none of them fled. Our forces remained concentrated from the village of Gorki, along the Semeyonovskii ravine, to the Old Smolensk Road, and were in full battle readiness to repel any further enemy attacks. The [French] were first to cease fire and therefore they were first to admit their exhaustion. Napoleon only had the Guard remaining in reserve while several regiments were not committed on our side. Prince Kutuzov prudently utilized his reserves and could still defend the ground to the last while maintaining good order. Napoleon let us withdraw to Mozhaisk without attempting any pursuit which, once again, demonstrated that he had broken his teeth on us, and was seemingly content that the battlefield was left to him to witness the immense casualties that his forces had suffered, especially in cavalry, the best cuirassier and dragoon regiments having been annihilated. This loss proved to be irreparable. It was here [on the field of Borodino] that the flower of the French army withered; it was here that the formidable conquerors of Europe were first broken.

The solemn prayer on the eve of the Battle of Borodino. (by E. Zaitsev)

The Burning of Moscow in September 1812. (German engraving based on drawing by Johan Rugendas, 1820)

The Grande Armée crossing the Niemen River in June 1812. (by Felician von Myrbach)

"Who will prevail?" (by V. Mazurowski)

The Grande Armée on the outskirts of Smolensk. (drawing by A. Adam)

"*Russian Infantry and French Cavalry: If a bayonet is not enough, here is a musket butt!*". (contemporary print by A. Venetsianov)

Prince Peter Bagration mortally wounded at Borodino. (painting by A. Vepkhadze)

"Seslavin's Discovery" – Alexander Seslavin (standing on the tree branch) observing the French army marching on Borovsk. Seslavin's discovery alerted the Russians that Napoleon had abandoned Moscow. (unknown artist, early 19th century)

Battle of Maloyaroslavets. (painting by P. von Hesse)

"An episode from the Patriotic War." In his memoirs, Radozhitskii did not shy away from describing atrocities that the Russian peasants committed against isolated enemy troops. (painting by I. Pryanishnikov)

Russian army liberating the city of Vyazma in November 1812. (by P. von Hesse)

"The Retreat". (painting by Jan Suchodolski)

Radozhitskii witnessed numerous human miseries during the pursuit of the retreating Grande Armée and described some of them in his memoirs. (British print by James Atkinson, 1813)

Francois Vendramini's portrait of Mikhail Golenischev-Kutuzov, published posthumously, remains one of the best contemporary portraits of the field marshal. It shows a scar in the temple area where an Ottoman musket ball struck Kutuzov, passing through his head and damaging his eye muscles.

General Peter Bagration, the fiery and impetuous Georgian prince, nicknamed "the Lion of the Russian army". (British engraving based on F. Vendramini's portrait, 1813)

General Mikhail Barclay de Tolly, courageous and prudent officer whose strategy of retreat was critical to the Russian victory over Napoleon in 1812. (British engraving based on F. Vendramini's portrait, 1813)

General Levin Gottlieb Bennigsen, Kutuzov's one-time friend later turned into a rival. (British engraving based on G. Dawe's portrait, 1820s)

Right: *The "Bayard of the Russian army," General Mikhail Miloradovich.* (portrait by George Dawe, 1820s)

Below: *Ataman Matvei Platov and Cossacks pursuing the retreating Grande Armée.* (German print based on the drawing by Gregorius von Schadow, 1813)

Denis Davydov commanded one of the many Russian flying detachments and later earned great fame with his memoirs. (Colored aquatint by M. Dubourg after Alexander Orlovsky's drawing, 1814)

Admiral Pavel Chichagov, commander of the Army of the Danube in 1812. He was largely blamed for the failure to intercept Napoleon on the shores of the Berezina. (portrait by unknown artist, possibly James Saxon)

General Aleksey Arakcheyev, who introduced important artillery reforms in the wake of the Russian defeats in 1805-1807. (portrait by George Dawe, 1820s)

Emperor Alexander of Russia

General Alexander Kutaisov, young, charismatic, and talented commander of the Russian artillery at Borodino. Carried away by his ardor, he joined the action and was killed. (portrait by George Dawe, 1820s)

Alexander Figner, young and ambitious artillery officer who commanded one of the flying detachments and earned notoriety for mistreating French prisoners. (Russian print based on a portrait by unknown artist, 1810s)

General Alexander Osterman-Tolstoy, experience and capable commander who distinguished himself at Ostrovno. Holding off Napoleon's attacks, he famously ordered his men to defend at all costs, "We will hold the ground and perish!". (by George Dawe, 1820s)

Aleksey Yermolov, gifted artillery officer who served as the chief of staff of the 1st Western Army. (by George Dawe, 1820s)

Peter Wittgenstein. He commanded the 1st Corps in 1812 and briefly led the combined Russo-Prussian forces in the spring of 1813. (German print by G. Lehmann, 1813)

FROM BORODINO TO MOSCOW

Napoleon had never before experienced a battle as murderous as Borodino. Considering the heavy losses among generals on both sides, this battle was literally a general one. Despite the enemy's numerical superiority, the Russians had never before fought with such ferocity as on this momentous occasion. The fallen front ranks were quickly replenished by the rear ranks. With hearts aching, they steadfastly endured all the damage inflicted by cannonballs and bullets, spreading death in the enemy ranks while suffering equally at their hands.

Despite Captain Figner's ardent desire to fight, the company was not sent into action. During the afternoon we were moved to the village of Gorki, from where we became witness to the horrors of war. When, following the enemy's capture of the *kurgan* lunette [the Great Redoubt], our troops concentrated in anticipation of another assault, General Miloradovich's adjutant came to us and led our company directly to the center, which by now had turned into the right flank of the battle line. We prepared for battle and cheered our soldiers, believing that we were about to enter the fight. But contrary to our expectations, the adjutant led us behind the dragoons and departed, leaving us there. While standing there we saw plenty of dead Russian soldiers and a destroyed artillery caisson that was surrounded by burnt ground and the charred remains of horses. To the left of us, about one hundred *sazhens* [700 feet] beyond the ditch, there were four horse-artillery guns that had been battered by enemy cannonballs. Only three cannoniers stood by each gun: all the rest were lying dead around them. In front of us, struck down by cannon shot or musket balls, dragoons were incessantly falling to the ground. We stood in a tight formation behind them, with the guns, all of them still limbered up as we were awaiting further orders, next to one another. Mounted on our horses, Figner and I were stationed one on each flank of the company (he - on the right, I - on the left) right opposite the enemy guns. Flying through the dragoons, cannon shot, shells, canister and even musket balls [regularly] reached our company and we lost several men and horses. It was then that I understood that there could be nothing worse during a battle than to remain idle under an enemy's bombardment. Every soldier traced the flight of each cannonball, and, in spite of themselves, paid respect to it. Turning my horse, I rode up to Figner and said, "It seems we are waiting in vain for orders! It would be better if we take position next to that horse artillery, and take matters into our hands..." Just at that moment, something suddenly flew past my left temple and knocked me off my horse. I fell unconscious on the ground and lay like dead for the next quarter of an hour. No one raised me because they believed that I had been killed. However, after a while, I started to regain consciousness and memory alike, and, finding myself lying on the ground, and tried to move. The cannoniers, noticing my motions, quickly came to my help. I wobbled as if in a haze, my wounded head kept falling from one shoulder to another and burning with extreme pain. I could not distinguish objects since everything spun around me and seemed enveloped in a fog. After a momentary respite, I was put on a horse and, embracing the horse's neck, rode in an unknown direction. My horse walked briskly, frequently stopping because of cannonballs bouncing on my right. Numerous killed and wounded lay on the ground, while, dodging the cannonballs, members of the Moscow *opolchenye* were picking up the survivors picked up and carrying them to the rear. Eventually, somehow finding myself on a road, I saw some *opolchenye* in the brush. Caring not for the battle, they sat together around a fire, over which hung a kettle. I asked them in a weak voice, where the wounded were cared for and one of them led me to the place. There were numerous unfortunates, with various types of injuries, all of them groaning and shouting. Especially frightening and pathetic was a certain Tatar with a black and ugly face of the type known as a Teptyarsk Cossack. As I arrived, [a surgeon] was extracting a bullet from behind his shoulder and the Tatar was writhing and screaming in a terrible fashion. A physician came up to me and helped me get off my horse. After examining my head, he made an ointment, placed a poultice on and bandaged me. Later I was told that I was knocked off the horse by a shell fragment that flew very close to my head: once again, then, I had suffered a contusion!

Meanwhile, Figner went to General Miloradovich and, pointing out that it had lost several gunners wounded and one officer killed without actually participating in the battle, informed him ofbthe disadvantageous position of his company. Since the French were not attempting anything of importance, and the battle was waning, he was therefore ordered to withdraw the company to the general park on the Mozhaisk road, where all the transports and disordered artillery companies were already being assembled. After getting bandaged, I rejoined my company just as it passed by. The French were not far from our rear and their cannonballs were still reaching the road along which our troops had started to withdraw. Even a minor attack in this direction would have caused profound disorder to our train since serried ranks of wagons crammed with wounded and healthy alike were making off with all the haste that they could muster. By dusk we had got beyond Mozhaisk, and spent the night in a field that, though small, was yet well hidden. But throughout the hours of darkness, I did not know what to do with my injured head, which was burning and making me rave as if I was feverish.

Anyone who has not experienced war would find it difficult to believe how far back n cannonballs can sometimes reach during a battle. On several occasions I observed enemy shot fly over entire lines and columns, only to hit, as if on target, solitary individuals and horses wandering behind the front, the consequence being that I always considered it more dangerous to be in the rear than the front. I occasionally witnessed how a single unintentional move or turn saved or exposed men to a deadly blow. Thus, this particular incident from the battle of Borodino was often told. Artillery Colonel V., standing with his company in reserve at the bivouacs at noon, ordered lunch to be served inside a tent where he sat with his officers to eat.

He sat on a drum while the rest lay on the ground. Cannonballs flew all around them but did not spoil the appetite of officers who continued to consume their meal. Suddenly, a six-pounder cannonball, at the end of its trajectory, bounced off the ground directly into the tent and landed on the colonel's leg, slightly touching his stomach. The blow appeared to be so weak that the colonel picked up the cannonball, rolled it among the plates and said jokingly: "Lads, here is a snack for you." His company remained in reserve throughout the battle. But during the evening the colonel suddenly began to feel pain in the stomach where the cannonball touched him. The pain continually intensified. The following day he suffered from an inflammation in his stomach and on the third day – he passed away. I heard an even more incredible story. An enemy shell struck a cavalryman's mount. Before the horse could fall to the ground, the shell exploded inside her stomach, and yet the trooper, though thrown into the air together with his saddle, survived unscathed. All of this sounds like a folktale but eyewitnesses assured us that these incidents actually happened. Thus, several enemy cannonballs fell directly into the muzzles of our guns. No wonder then that, with so many projectiles flying in all direction, they oftentimes collided and bounced back, striking their own troops.

It was said that at the beginning of the battle, an eagle soared above Prince Kutuzov's head. The Prince, taking off his hat, supposedly welcomed it as a harbinger of victory. But many of us doubted that the Commander-in-Chief would have preoccupied himself with an eagle at a time when all his thoughts and attention were focused on the battlefield. In all probability, the eagle's random appearance during the battle struck some people as foretelling something important. But we cannot discount the possibility that shrewd generals [like Kutuzov] are eager to exploit even the slightest incidents to inspire their soldiers. Thus, Napoleon, wishing to convince his soldiers of an imminent victory, exclaimed at the sun rise on the day of Borodino, "Here is the Sun of Austerlitz!" And yet, he was bitterly mistaken.

FROM BORODINO TO MOSCOW

At nightfall, our troops moved to the edge of the forest, while the French remained in positions that they had occupied, and made no attempt to pursue us. It was said that they had even retreated for four *verstas* [2.6 miles] from the battlefield, but very few believed this claim since Napoleon was not defeated and in fact had in part driven us back. Besides, if it were true, Prince Kutuzov would not have retreated. That said, the enemy's partial victory only produced cold and hunger on a battle field drenched in the blood of courageous warriors and that after such tremendous effort. That's where the essence of military glory lay in the eyes of a philosopher!

At dawn on 27 August [8 September], our troops began to retreat to Mozhaisk, stopping beyond the town. That day Napoleon dispatched his cavalry to pursue us, and even then the pursuit was light, without the slightest pressure. At night we broke our camp at Mozhaisk and continued to retreat to the village of Zemlino. The French immediately took Mozhaisk following a light skirmish with the rearguard which was placed under the command of General Miloradovich.

At dawn, as we marched through abandoned villages along the main road, we encountered numerous soldiers from the Moscow *opolchenie* bustling around huge kettles filled with porridge and potato. These warriors slept through the morning and did not have time to prepare or eat food. Wherever we encountered them, we found them either around kettles or resting on hills. Our exhausted and hungry soldiers called these scum locusts. One *opolchenie* warrior recognized a fellow countryman among the gunners in our company and began to tell him how in the last battle they charged the French. "At first," he said, "we advanced briskly since no bullets were fired at us. But the wily French let us come closer to the brushwood and then fired cannon and muskets so forcefully that we fled in all directions. Their uhlans then charged us. We would have all been killed if not for Matvei Ivanovich [Platov] and his Cossacks, who came just in time to save us. He, our beloved and may the Lord grant him good health, shouted to us, "Get away from here while you are still alive!"

- and then charged the French with his Cossacks. In this fashion the Cossacks saved us and we went back to picking up the wounded."

Our troops continued to retreat, reaching the village of Krutitsa on the Nara River. The French tried to ford the river. The determination of our rearguard, in front of almost the entire army, [produced] a rather fierce combat. The [French Imperial] Guard, which was not involved in the battle at Borodino, wanted to distinguish itself during the pursuit, but General Miloradovich's prudent orders limited the enemy attacks. We even had the pleasure of seeing dozens of soldiers from Napoleon's [Imperial] Guards taken prisoner and driven past us by Cossacks. They were tall and slender men with gallant faces, dressed in fashionable blue uniforms with red lapels, and tall bearskin caps with white tassels on their heads.

Meanwhile, my head felt better. A skilled physician from our brigade produced a life-saving lotion that soon ended both the inflammation and the headache. A better diet, movement and clean air only further helped me overcome the fever. With my head bandaged, I was able to ride my horse. Though the injury I suffered in the left temple was not as strong as the one endured to my leg, I still felt frequent dizziness and fainting; worst of all, meanwhile, it profoundly affected my memory. Such is the frailty of a human being! Not even a blow but just a touch of condensed air rendered me unconscious. I can state that during those fifteen minutes of unconsciousness, I did not inhabit this world, as if I was dead.

Chapter VI

From Moscow to Tarutino

On 30 August [11 September] we arrived at a fortified camp established around the village of Mamonova, some 19 *verstas* [13 miles] from Moscow. Picturesque hills crowned with groves and beautiful manor houses were half visible above the tree tops, signaling that we were already in the environs of our ancient capital which flourished peacefully in the quiet countryside and had not seen any enemy forces since the time of Otrepyev.[1] 28 And yet now everyone sought to destroy it! We looked with sadness at the surroundings that were about to be ravaged by military disasters. As we approached the heart of the Russian realm, we bowed our heads, ashamed to look at the golden- domed mother city that we could not protect from destruction. The deadly weapons in the hands of our soldiers seemed utterly useless and our strength impotent against the triumphant enemy who trampled our Christian kingdom. Many feeble minds embraced the idea of Napoleon's supernatural abilities. He was widely cursed in the churches and some know-it-alls even claimed that his name was mentioned in the Apocalypse [Book of Revelation]. Many Russian warriors, who scorned the horrors of death, were becoming physically and mentally distressed.

---

1 It is generally believed that Gregory Otrepyev was an impostor who claimed, during the Times of Troubles, to be the youngest son of Tsar Ivan the Terrible. Supported by Polish troops, he successfully claimed the throne and was crowned as Tsar in July 1605. Less than a year later a conspiracy of Russian nobles overthrew him, causing the start of violent civil strife that last until 1613. In 1610 Polish forces occupied much of Russia, including Moscow.

THE RUSSIAN CAMPAIGN OF 1812

The following day we stopped just 4 four *verstas* [2.6 miles] from the capital. Our troops encamped in battle positions on the Vorobyevo [Sparrow] Hills and redoubts were constructed along the front line. We expected that there would be a decisive battle, more ferocious than Borodino. Golden-domed Moscow stretched as far as the eye could see and seemingly appealed to her sons to defend her. The very sight of this beautiful and ancient capital of the Russian realm inspired our soldiers and instilled them with reckless gallantry. Despite the soldiers' grim faces, it was apparent that every one of them was ready to die defending his fatherland, thus upholding the last glory and grandeur of the Russian people. But circumstances produced a rather different and unexpected outcome.

In this general agitation of spirit and mind on the edge of the abyss about to claim our Fatherland, no one chose to remain uninvolved. My comrades and all the other officers had been very contemplative, rarely uttering a word since no one could fully express what he felt. Our company commander, Captain Figner, was often consumed by this gloomy silence more than anyone else and was frequently so distracted that he could not listen to reports submitted to him. He rode absent-mindedly on horseback and let me take charge of the company.

Feelings woken by the sight of the doomed capital, as well as by the hatred felt toward our enemy, excited my imagination. Already affected by the contusion so powerfully as this was, one morning I experienced a genuinely patriotic dream. I dreamt that I somehow found myself disguised as a Frenchman in the enemy camp, where I carried loaded pistols in my pockets in order to assassinate Napoleon. I went to a redoubt by a battery where I saw a general leaning against the ramparts and observing the deployment of our army through a spyglass. He was surrounded by officers whose reverent attitude toward this general convinced me that it was Napoleon himself. I immediately took a pistol out of my pocket and shot the general from the side: the bullet pierced his chest and the general fell to the

FROM MOSCOW TO TARUTINO

ground. But as he did, he turned his face to me and, to my grief, I saw that it was not Napoleon. "Ugh, it's Murat," I exclaimed, as I was grasped by officers who would certainly have shot me if I had not woken up.

On the morning of 1 [13] September Figner had gone somewhere but when he returned to the company I told him about my dream. He laughed and, among other things, mentioned that he recently had the very same dream. He then told me that to calm his tumultuous thoughts, he traveled to Moscow to pray. Figner seemed to be quite devout since he always wore a small icon of St. Nicholas the Wonderworker on his chest under the uniform. He wore a uniform made from thick cloth of the sort supplied to the rank and file with [the Order of] St. George hanging through a buttonhole. He received this medal for his exploits at Ruse in Moldavia. At this time, his hair was unkempt and his beard unshaved, and he looked like a desperate common soldier. In this dishevelled state, Figner prayed eagerly inside an empty church. A local sexton [*dyachok*], upon seeing a soldier kneeling and crying in front of the icon of St. Nicholas the Wonderworker, and not understanding what caused his anguish, approached Figner and told him compassionately, "It seems, soldier, you are experiencing great hardship, so take this small token." He then gave him a bronze coin. Having finished his prayer, Figner stood up, looked at the sexton and gave him a silver ruble with the words "Here, take this larger token!" He then mounted his horse and galloped away, leaving the sexton thunderstruck by the poor soldier's incredible generosity and unable to comprehend the marvels that had unfolded in front of his very eyes. Meanwhile, Figner told me that, in the wake of this incident he had rifdden the full length of our battle position and noticed again that our left flank was weaker, just as it was at Borodino. He immediately wrote a report on this matter and wanted to deliver it to the Field Marshal [Kutuzov] in order to expose what Figner believed was concealed from him. In his report he explained that, in all of the previous campaigns, the weakness

THE RUSSIAN CAMPAIGN OF 1812

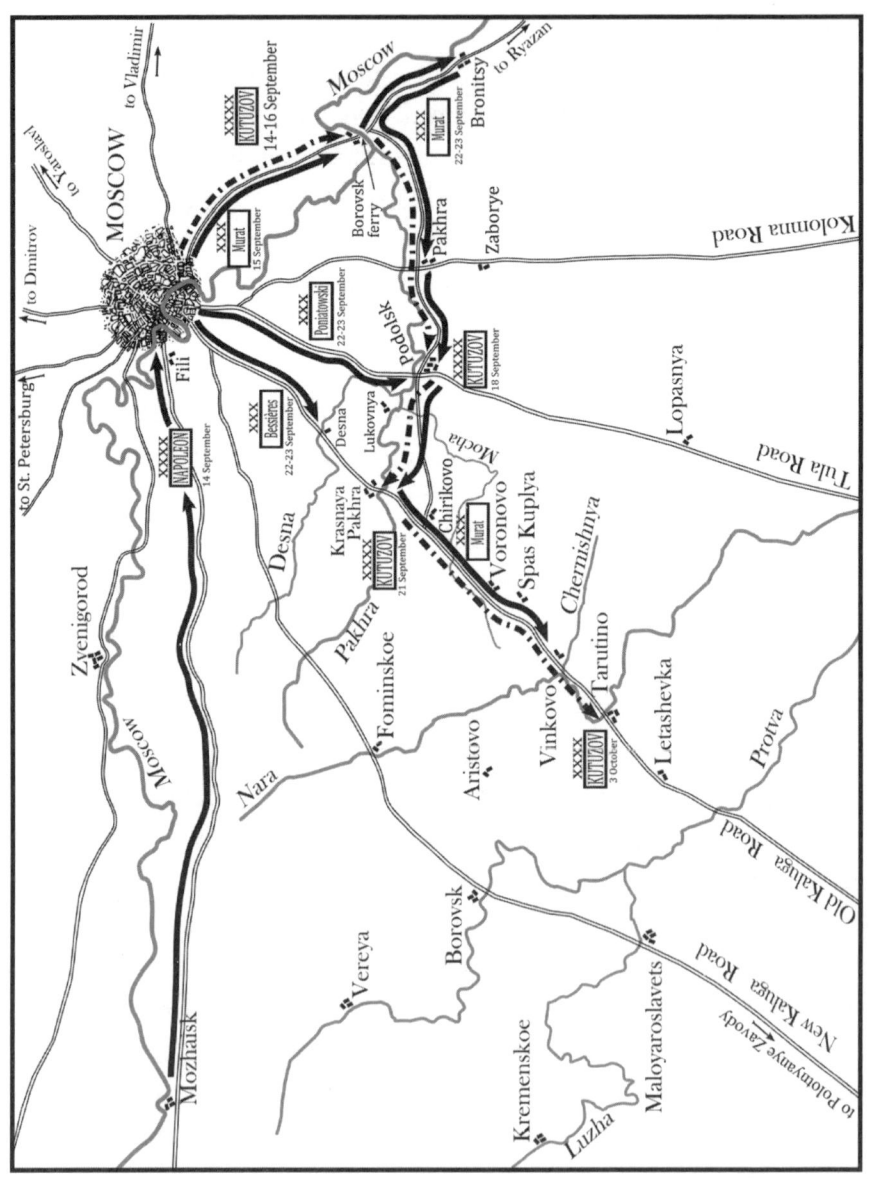

The Fall of Moscow and Kutuzov's Tarutino March-Maneuver.

of the left flank of our army had allowed the enemy to direct his main forces against it and achieve clear victories. After completing a final version of his observations, Figner shaved and tidied himself before travelling to the main headquarters. He was driven by a certain enthusiasm.

Meanwhile, the headquarters held a council of war attended by all senior generals. The Field Marshal made the decision to withdraw his troops and abandon Moscow to the [French] – so they could perish there. Only Field Marshal Prince Kutuzov, the true son of Russia who was suckled on her breast milk [*vskormlennyi eye sostsami*], could surrender the ancient capital of the empire without a fight. Public opinion would have condemned any other commander as an apparent traitor, but a great sacrifice for the salvation of the whole nation was acceptable if it was offered by the Farherland's chosen, not to mention foremost, defender.

In the evening Figner returned to our camp and gladly recounted how the Field Marshal received him caringly, even though it was difficult to get access to him, and graciously listened to his military observations, thanked him for his effort, treated him kindly and promised to employ him in *some important cause* [author's emphasis]. Figner told us [Kutuzov's] Chief of Staff, Alexey Petrovich Yermolov, had helped him the most in gaining access to the Field Marshal. Figner extolled this general and called him "the Shield of the Fatherland."

Our troops departed during the night of 2 [14] September. To mislead the enemy and prevent him from threatening our flank, we were ordered to march through Moscow. At dawn, our 4th Corps was the last, marching in the wake of the army toward Moscow. The rearguard, under the command of General Miloradovich, remained in place to delay the French. Our retreat was conducted in an orderly fashion but surrounded by dreary silence. Approaching the bereaved capital, the mother of all Russian cities, our soldiers gazed with broken hearts at the beautiful buildings that were being abandoned to the enemy: the Pashkov palace with its peculiar architectural features, numerous large and beautiful houses, the Kremlin with its gothic [*goticheskimi*] towers, the vast and ancient palaces of the Russian tsars and the golden-domed [bell-tower] of Ivan the Great,[2] all of them were silent witnesses to impending calamity. Everything was now sacrificed to the enemy! And all the while, thousands of Russians fled with the arms in their hands! Such upsetting thoughts caused us indescribable grief: our hearts, indeed, were aching so much that we shed tears. The despair of the unfortunate residents of [Moscow] only further depressed us. At every step we encountered poignant scenes: women, elders, and children crying and wailing, not knowing where to go; pale and frantic people bustling in and out of the houses without understanding what they should do. Everything they knew was about to be destroyed, the Antichrist himself was approaching and Doomsday nigh... Our courageous warriors shuddered at the sight of the moribund capital of their fatherland. Bustling movement, noise of [troops] passing by, the darkness of an autumn day and dreadful thoughts about the approaching enemy served as portents of the horrors about to befall Moscow.

Both generals and officers, and soldiers walked dejectedly, the only thing that revived our spirits a little being the priests who stood in front of every church wearing their full vestments, and both blessing the passing soldiers with the holy cross and sprinkling them with holy water. While the troops marched along the waterfront between the Kremlin wall and the river, the commander-in-chief of the 1st Army [Barclay de Tolly] stood near the Stone Bridge to maintain order.

We passed by the Kremlin and entered the city, where we saw misery, crying and despair everywhere. Officers began to gather in groups to discuss what would happen next since none of us knew

---

2 The Ivan the Great Bell Tower is the tallest of the towers (81 m or 266 ft) in the Moscow Kremlin complex and was built in 1508 for the Russian Orthodox cathedrals in Cathedral Square. The Bell Tower is named after Ivan III the Grand prince of Moscow and all Rus (r. 1462-1505).

what to expect. Meanwhile, under the pretext of fetching water, the rank and file slipped into nearby shops, houses and cellars that had been left open as if to treat the passersby, and, while there, bade goodbye [in their own manner] to Mother Moscow...

Just before the barrier, we reached a wide street crammed with rows of carts. Carriages and wagons moved with artillery alongside both sides of the street. One could observe a bizarre mixture of people of all ranks and transports of all types. The wagons were filled with trunks, bundles and feather pillows on which servants sat, while footmen walked behind them, leading horses and hounds. It seemed that, despite their hurry to flee, everyone was taking their favorite possessions. Some transports were forcing others out of the line, so Figner allowed many of them to follow his guns until the city was left behind. The infantry had separated from us to march through roundabout streets. Beyond the barrier, the entire road and fields were littered with all sorts of carriages, people, horses, and dogs, all hurrying in the wake of the army along the Ryazan road. About three *verstas* [2 miles] from the city, the civilian residents began to separate from us and, little by little, they scattered along the country roads.

By nightfall we approached the village of Panki, about 15 *verstas* [10 miles] from Moscow. It was then that we saw fire in the city. It was only the beginning. The fire intensified throughout the night and by the morning of 3 [15] September a greater part of the horizon was enveloped in flames. The fiery waves ascended to the heavens and thick black smoke curled across the sky, and even reached us. We involuntarily shuddered with surprise and horror. The superstitious, not comprehending what was happening before their eyes, thought that the fall of Moscow signaled the fall of Russia, the triumph of the Antichrist, the impending start of Judgement Day and the demise of the world. Our sense of bewilderment was soon replaced by the feeling of anger: "Here is golden-domed Moscow! Shine our dear city, the capital of Russia!" the soldiers murmured with great vexation.

As the sun set, Figner approached me, "Hey, brother Ilya! I want to say goodbye to you, I am going back to Moscow. If I do not return within a week, do not consider me alive. I asked General Yermolov to let you command the company in my absence." He shook my hand and disappeared. His words astounded me as much as the Moscow fire did. His statement "I am going back to Moscow. If I do not return within a week, do not consider me alive" was a great mystery to me

After resting on 3 [15] September, we resumed our march on the Ryazan road the following day. The flames of the burning capital licked the sky while swirling smoke soared up high, forming thick black clouds. The weather was overcast, cold and wet, rather appropriate for the current situation.

During this march I had the honor of meeting Field Marshal Prince Kutuzov. Marching on a country road, I encountered a rivulet where I had to move my cannon across a frail bridge that had been loosened by all of the infantry and artillery that had moved across before us. After examining the steep riverbanks I noticed this problem and, unwilling to endanger [my] cannon, I returned to the main road in order to march a bit further and find a safer place to cross. The Field Marshal, riding in a covered carriage, noticed my retrograde movement and called to me, asking what I was doing. I explained what had happened and he ordered one of his column guides [staff officers] to lead my artillery by the most convenient and closest roads to our division. As I spoke with the prince, I observed his eminent and calm face. He seemed to be fully convinced of the impending change in the enemy's fortune and expected only success to crown prudent decisions that he had undertaken to save the fatherland.

After crossing the rivulet, I joined the infantry. We passed by beautiful manor houses and villages that were located on the Moscow River. Everything here was empty and abandoned. Artillery had to move through the orchards and past long greenhouses lined with lemon and [bitter] orange trees that were laden with near ripe fruits I walked inside the greenhouse, enjoying its greenery but saddened to see numerous overturned vats and pots, broken trees and shattered glass. Thus, the war was destroying exquisite undertakings in the heart of our fatherland.

The march proved to be some fifteen *verstas* [10 miles] long. After crossing the Moscow River on a bridge at the Borovskii ferry, we took battle positions along the heights of the limestone riverbank. Standing on these hills, we could clearly see our burning capital. Just as we set up our bivouacs, we heard a terrible explosion from a gunpowder magazine in the city. The explosion was so powerful that it shook the entire vicinity and spread in a thunderous rumble beyond the horizon. At that moment I momentarily remembered Figner and his last words…

Continuing our retreat, we made a sudden turn to the right, that is to southwest, on 5 [17] September and marched along the Pakhra River, passing by Nikitsk and bivouacking in front of the Frolovskii pit.

Proceeding along the Pakhra, we reached the town of Podolsk on 6 [18] September. The generals occupied apartments in the town while the troops camped on both sides of the road about one *versta* away from the town. It was [cool] autumn weather, the ground was wet and naked. While soldiers set up their tents and gathered firewood, the officers suffered from the cold. Fortunately, we had ample amounts of bread, meat, vodka and oats since we were given plenty of everything in Moscow. The only challenge was finding hay for our horses. To our great joy, the Podolsk Treasury still possessed considerable quantities of copper coins that the local authorities did not know what to do with and ultimately decided to distribute among the troops. Each regiment and artillery company was required to send a squad [*komanda*] to receive whatever amount was allocated to it. So, my company also received its due in coins.

We had spent all our money on our march from Vilna and owed money to sutlers. Having no money, we thought that, following the loss of Moscow, we were not going to receive our salary at all and so this meager gift was very helpful.

Meanwhile, for six days and six nights Moscow slowly died, turning to ashes. The flames that consumed it left an indelible impression on the minds and feelings of, not only the sons of Russia, but the enemy as well. Its destruction shocked Russia and the whole of Europe alike, and affected many countries around the world. From the moment [Moscow] turned to ash, political upheavals gradually spread on both continents [Old and New World]. Thus, in six days the city that grew and thrived for six centuries disappeared. Its golden domed churches that once proudly ascended toward the sky, were now in ruins. Exquisite works of architecture, works of science and art were devastated. The joys and pleasures of luxurious living were claimed by the ashes. Only the Kremlin and its towers survived to witness the horrors [of the fiery destruction] and to convey them for posterity. The fire of Moscow is a landmark, even in world history, and the most glorious disaster in the history of Russia. Hardly can another such event be found throughout the distant antiquity of the past while, with the spread of literacy and the consequent softening of manners, modern times do not present any other example of such an extreme patriotic sacrifice. The man who, out of love of his Fatherland, struck the first spark that led to the fiery destruction of the capital, or was the main cause of this glorious sacrifice, was truly a Russian in spirit and heart. The glory of his name will only grow in the memories of future generations.

On 7 [19] September, we made a brief march and bivouacked beyond the woods. The Field Marshal's main headquarters moved to the village of Krasnaya Pakhra. Light cannon were again distributed between the regiments. I, together with four cannon, was assigned to the Pernovskii Regiment. But because of Figner's absence, I continued commanding the entire artillery company and therefore had to visit the company's other cannon that were assigned to the Yeletskii and Polotskii Regiments.

Without understanding the [purpose of our] flanking maneuver and not seeing any enemy forces, many thought that peace negotiations had been launched. There were even rumors that the Russian government had agreed to surrender all those provinces, including the town of Smolensk that Napoleon passed on his way to the Dnieper River, and to provide an auxiliary corps to attack English possessions in India. Either because of these rumors or maybe because the image of smoldering Moscow was still fresh in our memories, a general discontent intensified among the troops, patriotic grumbling increasing to such a degree as to warrant the attention of the supreme command.

To soothe the sons of Russia who were distraught by the loss of the capital, the person who was the direct target of soldiers' resentments as the initiator of this endless retreat and the cause of our heavy losses, decided to appear in front of the troops. His face was calm, convinced of the justice of his cause. Anyone familiar with a Russian soldier knows that one good word from the commander raises his confidence and lifts his spirit. So Commander of the 1st Army Barclay de Tolly passed in front of the lines of troops and, stopping in front of each regiment, made a brief but powerful and inspiring speech. I happened to be with the Yeletskii Regiment when this venerable General appeared alone in front of the soldiers in a modest uniform without any marks of distinction or orders and, stopping close to them, gave this memorable speech: "Brave warriors! Faithful sons of Russia! I see sadness on your faces. I see the sorrow that torments your hearts. I hear your voice of patriotic indignation. The current circumstances are, of course, unfortunate for every Russian but we are nowhere near the end of this campaign. Oftentimes, in the midst of extreme challenges, great sacrifices are needed for great results. Remember how Emperor Peter I once found himself in circumstances that were similar to ours. Remember how he led the enemy to Poltava, where he destroyed him. With the help of the Lord, and through your bravery, we hope to accomplish the same, if only you will patiently and calmly accept the will of your commanders who are leading you toward the salvation of the Fatherland and your own glory. It is true that our capital has turned to ash, but you must know that from these ashes has been born the destruction of the enemy and all of his forces. The enemy's troops are exhausted by deprivations and challenges of the prolonged campaign. They have lost half their men, and are disordered and demoralized, nothing but a mob of vagabonds who are hungry for food and plunder. Soon we will witness the destruction of the new Charles XII: he will try to flee from you faster than lightning but will only find death in the Russian realm whereupon his ashes will be scattered under your feet!" The last words were spoken with such expressiveness and passion that the soldiers seemed struck to their very hearts.

By speaking thus in front of each regiment, our venerable leader made peace with the warriors. His speech had an even more powerful effect when, in each case, he promoted several distinguished soldiers to the rank of non-commission officer and distributed several insignia of the Military Order of St. George for courage. In the Yeletskii Regiment alone, he promoted 20 soldiers to non-commissioned officer rank.

Soldiers quickly recovered their spirits. Old veterans with [long] mustaches] recalled stories of how their [grand]fathers had indeed crushed the Swedes at Poltava, and thought that Napoleon would share Charles XII's fate if only they would trust completely in their commanders' will and stand firmly to the last drop of their blood. Men no longer grieved for Moscow, saying that our tsar [Alexander I] could turn any town into a capital just as Peter the Great had turned swamps into St. Petersburg. By evening bands were playing in all the regiments and the sound of singing marked the resumption of the soldiers' revels. Calm weather, the pleasant glow of the sun setting beyond the horizon, the sound of music echoing through the woods, the fact that the trees obscured the smoke rising from devastated Moscow, comforting conversations, an uplifting hope in the future, and complete trust in the Field Marshal's orders: all of these soothed the hearts of warriors, and, [in hindsight], left me feeling better than I had for the entire campaign.

Having turned his troops to the Tula road, the Field Marshal suddenly transformed his withdrawal into an offensive movement that threatened the enemy's rear. He let the French march toward the northern provinces while he moved south and protected communications with the armies of Tormasov and Chichagov. More importantly, he protected the bountiful southern provinces that provided him with everything he needed to continue the campaign. Thus, with this single simple maneuver, our skilled commander brought great advantages to the Russian army, and frustrated and confused his opponent's entire strategy. Who would not recognize the superiority of this Russian Fabius?[3] Which son of Russia, with awe in his heart, would not consider him the true savior of the Fatherland?

In hindsight, even a common soldier cannot but marvel at the mistakes committed by the great Napoleon, blinded as he was by his own success. He seemed to have been so fixed on Moscow that he forgot all the rules of war. His first mistake was that, having established the base for his operations, he then ignored it and proceeded from Smolensk to Moscow, which turned into the fiery source for all of his sufferings. His second error was that at Borodino he got carried away by the bloody slaughter of the battle and lost an opportunity to direct all of his forces along the Old Smolensk Road. [Third mistake was that Napoleon marched straight to Moscow.] He could have sent cavalry alone, perhaps supported by an infantry corps, along the [main] road, while directing the remaining forces though Vereya and Borovsk, so as to maintain a flanking movement against our left wing, which would have allowed him to have access to the southern provinces and thereby provide his forces with all their necessities. He would have also separated our army from the armies of Tormasov and Chichagov. After capturing the southern provinces, he could have anticipated us at Moscow by several days and captured the town since our 90,000-man-strong army was not in any condition

---

3 Quintus Fabius Maximus Verrucosus Cunctator (ca. 280 BC – 203 BC) was a Roman politician and general, who commanded a Roman army against Hannibal during the Second Punic War. His agnomen Cunctator means "delayer" in Latin, and refers to his methodical operations against the Carthaginians.

to resist his 150,000 men. As a result we would certainly have been forced to march to Vladimir or Yaroslavl.

Instinctively confident in the blindness of his opponent, Field Marshal Kutuzov had not considered it necessary to protect the roads to Vereya during his retreat from Mozhaisk. But he could have left cavalry, with an infantry corps, to lure Napoleon to Moscow, while he marched toward the southern provinces. But such a movement would have been difficult to conceal from Napoleon, who could have guessed its purpose, captured Moscow and made the necessary adjustments to his military operations. The Field Marshal may have foreseen such dangers and thought it best not to alert [Napoleon] to his blindness, and instead led him to the gates of Moscow, only, by a sudden maneuver, to astonish and confuse him.

On 8 [20] September we continued to circle round Moscow, marching from the Tula road to the Kaluga route. Everyone now understood that we were moving into the enemy rear, so all and sundry increased their marching rate in the hope of catching the enemy off guard; the soldiers [even] lamented that the marches were not longer.

On 10 [22] September, the troops took up battle positions at Krasnaya Pakhra, where they remained calmly and quietly resting until the 13th. Confident that the enemy was dumbfounded [by our maneuver] everyone expected major consequences from the Field Marshal's prudent decisions. The first successes appeared soon thereafter. Every day we saw 200 or 300 French marauders, captured by Cossacks in nearby villages. Among them were even [Imperial] Guard, tall fellows, and officers in elegant uniforms. We were pleased to see that entire detachments of these terrible enemies, from whom we had kept constantly retreating, were not captured without bloodshed: it seemed that the spirit of vengeance was born out of the ashes of burned Moscow and began to spread death among its destroyers.

In three days over one thousand prisoners were brought to our army. They were kept outside our camp, disarmed but wearing their uniforms. It was fascinating to watch these man in diverse uniforms: a blue hussar standing next to crimson lancer; a tall cuirassier, wearing a helmet befitting a knight, towering over skinny Italian infantrymen; an [Imperial] Guard gunner, in a marten's cap [*kun'ya shapka*], looking contemptibly at short Westphalians; a Frenchman [stood next to] a Dutchman, a Spaniard with a Pole, a Bavarian with an Italian: what a strange brew of European nations in a single crowd. They themselves were surprised at their convergence, many of them not understanding each other as at the Tower of Babel, and only a few words of the language of the dominant nation [French] confirmed that they are all followers of the same destructive genius [Napoleon]. At noon, they were given their daily ration. A number, not being hungry yet, appeared reluctant to accept this meager gift. Others, for all that their pride was hurt and their feelings distressed, still obeyed the necessity. Of these last, some, hungry and driven by natural impulse to save their lives, quickly licked up the flour with their tongues until their mouths could hold no more and swallowed it dry, while others wrapped the flour in rags as if it was a precious jewel, or baked small [flat bread] cakes in hot ashes. Still wearing their uniforms as they were, one and all felt that accepting a handful of flour, and, still worse, a gift from the enemy, in order to survive, brought home the reality of their wretched existence. Many of them had various bronze and silver items - rings, earrings, and other jewelry - that they had plundered in Moscow. These they traded for food, and our good soldiers exchanged them for bread and biscuits, or bought with money that which they could have simply taken away from these plunderers as not belonging to them.

Meanwhile, we received good news that General Dorokhov,[4] who was dispatched with a detachment to the Mozhaisk road, had

---

4 Ivan Dorokhov (1762-1815). At the start of the campaign Dorokhov commanded the advance guard of the 4th Infantry Corps of the 1st Western Army and successfully escaped Napoleon's entrapment. He later commanded a cavalry rearguard of the combined Russian armies, distinguished himself leading cavalry charges at Borodino, and, after the abandonment of Moscow, took charge of a separate cavalry detachment comprised of the Elisavetgradskii Hussars, Life-Guard Dragoons, and three Cossack regiments, with two horse artillery cannon.

appeared in the enemy's rear, captured several thousand prisoners, burnt down the enemy [supply] park, intercepted mail and couriers, and seized eight *puds* [288 pounds] of stolen silver that was being transported from Moscow to Smolensk.

The French, preoccupied with the burning of Moscow, its looting and the subsequent division of plunder, seemed to have forgotten about us, or were so blinded by their imaginary victory that they triumphantly expected the conclusion of peace. Only later did they come to their senses. Thus, seeing no delegations coming from us to beg for mercy, they sent patrols along various roads seeking our army, which last, to their surprise, they found in their own rear, not far from Krasnaya Pakhra.

On 13 [25] September, the enemy departed from the town of Podolsk, threatening a flank of our army's battle position. To prevent them from reaching the Tula road and protect his right flank, at 3 o'clock in the afternoon the Field Marshal dispatched the 4th Infantry Corps and the 2nd Cavalry Corps to Podolsk under the command of Count Osterman-Tolstoy, to the same place. No sooner had we passed some fifteen *verstas* [10 miles], we encountered the enemy whom we had not seen in a long time. Upon seeing us, the French approached us, but we kept deploying into and out of columns, while all of the time using these manoeuvres to retreat without firing a single shot until halting for the night not far from the village of Aleksandrovo.

The following day the troops changed their positions and, still maneuvering, retreated for about eight more *verstas* [5.3 miles], once again without any shots fired. The enemy, it seemed, was unaware of our precise forces and acted very cautiously, also maneuvering and gradually reducing the distance between us. By nightfall they bivouacked just three *verstas* [2 miles] from us. Meanwhile, the main headquarters of our army moved out of Krasnaya Pakhra and retreated along the Kaluga road to the village of Babenkovo.

On the morning of 15 [27] September, our corps resumed their retreat and, after marching for another five *verstas* [3.3 miles], occupied a position near the village of Nemchinina The infantry and artillery were deployed at the edge of the woods. In front of us stretched a small valley, concealed by woods. To the right, General Paskevich's division stood in front of the village of Sashino, while on the left, the army's rearguard under command of General Miloradovich stood on the Kaluga road. Thick woods separated us from both Paskevich and Miloradovich. The Bashkirs and some dragoons were scattered in front of us. They lured the enemy flankers out of the woods that concealed the enemy's main forces from us. The weather was overcast and humid, and [despite the late season,] the trees were still green. At 4 o'clock in the afternoon the enemy columns came out of woods in front of the right flank of our line and the skirmishers began fire. We particularly liked watching various tricks and deceptions that the Bashkirs, who wore caps with ear-flaps and fired arrows like Cupids, resorted to as they buzzed around the French chasseurs, charging, retreating and luring them into ambushes before gathering again into a group, charging with screams and then scattering once more. Wrapped in his cloak [*burka*], Count Osterman-Tolstoy stood with a menacing face next to my guns and waited for the enemy's decisive movement. He seemed angry that the enemy acted cautiously. The enemy skirmishers and the Bashkirs continued to play around [*shutit*] until evening, with neither side suffering any losses. Meanwhile, we could hear a cannonade from the right. The enemy was attacking General Paskevich's division there. Some four *verstas* [2.6 miles] ahead and to the left of us was the corps of Prince Poniatowski. In order not to reveal his dispositions, the enemy did without camp-fires, everything therefore suggesting that he was observing the utmost caution.

The following day we marched just three *verstas* [2 miles], with the French following us. We crossed the Mocha Rivulet at the village of Okulovo in the evening and advanced for about a *versta* toward the village of Voronovo that was located on the Kaluga road. There we found another advantageous position along the edge of the woods. The woods in front of our line on the right flank were occupied by the jagers and dragoons. The left flank moved closer to General Miloradovich's rearguard while Paskevich's division stood next to our right flank..

We remained in this position on 17 [29] September. We heard a strong cannonade on our left flank, where the main army's rearguard was engaged in a fierce battle. While the King of Naple's cavalry engaged our forces, Prince Poniatowski advanced with his corps toward Voronovo, where he was defeated by General Miloradovich.

Our forces remained quiet until noon. Around 4 o'clock in the afternoon, the enemy then began deploying his cavalry columns on the other side of an elevated bank of the Mocha rivulet. Having first observed us for almost an hour without attempting anything, they then began to descend toward the our side of the valley on our side, initially a half squad of cavalry, then a full squad, then a squadron and then the whole mass, but without supporting this movement with any artillery. We allowed them to approach in good order to a distance of some 200 *sazhens* before suddenly opening fire from all our batteries along the entire line. In just a few moments we disrupted the entire tactical arrangement of the enemy cavalry, which fled quickly across the river, greatly amusing us.

It was said that while the enemy cavalry was parading in front of us, General [Gratien] Ferrier and his adjutant from the King of Naples' staff, went deep into the woods and started to record our deployment. Suddenly a non-commissioned officer of the Pskovskii Dragoon Regiment, who was hidden behind a tree, jumped out with a pistol in hand and aiming it against the general's chest, shouted in a terrible voice, "Halt, pardon!" The general and adjutant were so preoccupied with their topography that they did not even manage to drop their pencils and grasp their swords. The dragoon, with comrades who came to his aid, had already seized them and rushed them toward the infantry lines.

It was apparent that the enemy did not have sufficient forces against us and therefore could not threaten us. So Count Osterman's 4th Corps was ordered to return to the main army. On 18 [30] September, we marched with General Paskevich's division and dragoons for some three *verstas* [2 miles] and joined General Miloradovich's rearguard on the Kaluga road.

At 5 o'clock in the afternoon on 20 September [1 October], Count Osterman's corps passed by the burning estate of Count Rostopchin in Voronovo. Our generals and officers stopped to observe this unusual sight since it was said that the count set this estate - his favorite place of residence where he nurtured his family's happiness - on fire with his own hand. I envisioned this famous patriot, with heavy heart, looking at the flames that devoured beautiful colonnades and their stony guardians, the centaurs. As he watched the present, it seemed that he had delved into the past and remembered delights that he had enjoyed just recently in times of peace. At all events, his heart burning for vengeance, and his glum forehead imprinted with bitterness ... the count left the following inscription on a column for the French: "I spent eight years this estate beautiful and living on it happily with my family. The inhabitants of the village fled their homes upon your approach, but I chose to burn my estate so as not to allow you to defile it by your very presence. In Moscow, I have abandoned two houses fully furnished with furniture worth one and a half million rubles, but here I leave you nothing but ashes!" Such a ferocity of Russian patriotism is worthy of a painter's elegant brush.

We followed the 4th Corps for about one *versta* beyond Voronovo before halting to support General Miloradovich's rear guard and maintain his communications with the main army.

On 21 September [2 October[, our forces retreated along the main road to the village of Tarutino, The enemy, discovering the actual direction of our army, united his forces and began to engage our rearguard more vigorously. We marched throughout the night. Having only poor bridges, the rivers posed considerable obstacles to us. The area around Voronovo was intersected with ravines and openings in the woods that, near the main road, became broad valleys, some two *verstas* [1.3 miles] wide that offered excellent opportunities for small detachments to check the enemy.

The following day, the rearguard stood firmly on the heights behind the village of Spas Kuplya, where it was supported by the 4th Corps. Starting at 1 pm, we were engaged in an intense fight with the French. It was here that I witnessed for the first time General Miloradovich's art of war and admired the orderliness with which he conducted all the movements of his troops. The columns moved as if on a chess board, the batteries maintained cross fire, the lines of skirmishers, supported by the reserves, pulled back without ceasing fire, while on both flanks, having waited in ambush, cavalry detachments made use of forest clearings to charge the enemy skirmishers and force them to fall back. The enemy was unable to move forward and was forced to deploy in columns, reinforce his cavalry charges and set up artillery batteries. All the while [French] attacks were countered by similarly resolute [Russian] defense. It was impossible not to admire this former associate of Suvorov's [Miloradovich] as he rode in the most calm and gallant of fashions in the midst of the hail of cannon shot and muskets; approached some gunner officer, and, pointing toward the enemy artillery, told him, "I command you to knock that battery out!"; or when he addressed a unit of infantrymen, shouting, "Soldiers! I give you this [enemy] column, take it!" Thus inspired, the soldiers charged, shouting "Hurrah!", and routed the enemy, while the cannon obeyed the voice of this hero and destroyed the enemy's batteries.

I, however, was unable to participate in this minor combat that was so noteworthy for the precision of its direction, simply remaining with my battery and keepimng between the infantry columns of the second line: from our entire brigade, only Lieutenant Colonel M.'s battery company took part in the fight. That said, enemy shells kept bursting in between my cannon albeit without causing any harm. The French, realizing the futility of their attempts to dislodge our rear guard, ended the battle at nightfall.

Chapter VII

From Tarutino to Maloyaroslavets

For almost two weeks (from 23 September to 5 October [5-17 October]), we lived quietly at the Tarutino camp, without concerning ourselves with the French. We were provided with recruits, horses, and ammunition, sheepskin coats, boots, and fed biscuits, while the horses received plenty of oats and hay. We also received tripled payments and, on top of it, the rank-and-file was given 5 rubles in *assignates* [paper money] for the battle of Borodino. Our camp overflowed with supplies as various provisions were delivered from southern Russian to the Tarutino camp. Stores were set up amidst our bivouacs offering all kinds of necessities to military men, and a bustling trade ensued. It was then that everyone truly went on a bender. Peasants from nearby and faraway settlements came to the camp to find their surviving relatives or fellow villagers. Peasant women came daily in droves, bringing goodies to soldiers and seeking their husbands, sons and brothers. I saw many such women, driven by militant patriotism and proclaiming, "Just give us, lord, pikes and we will go after the French ourselves." It seemed that all of Russia had converged spiritually at the Tarutino camp, and every true son of the fatherland, even those living in the most remote corners of the country, rushed here, if not in person then with his heart and spirit, sacrificing their last possessions [for the sacred cause]. All that was deemed precious for the whole empire was confined to this camp - the last bastion of Russia. The last hopes of the perishing fatherland rested on the military commander's prudent vision. No other Russian [military] leader seemed as important and towered in the eyes of the whole nation as Prince Kutuzov. All of Russia gazed at him and the fate of the empire depended on the execution of his plans. But the prince was the native son of Russia, nurtured on her bosom, feeling unwavering love toward her. The fate of the fatherland was very close to his heart and he treasured the trust of the monarch and the nation. Hiding behind modest appearances in his camp, he slyly snared the impatient enemy before his experienced mind finally triumphed over Fortune's proud pet [Napoleon] and the once invincible turned into the vanquished.

[After the war] some claimed that hunger and cold were our main allies in the destruction of France. But what about the Field Marshal's skill in bringing the enemy to such an extreme condition and exploiting even natural disasters for this purpose? How can we not be grateful to this commander's prudence with which he deceived Napoleon's arrogant expectation for a favorable peace? How clever were the rumors spread among the enemy army that our army was in the midst of miserable conditions and suffering extreme disadvantages in everything; that the veteran soldiers remained only in the front ranks and the rest of the army comprised recruits and *opolchenye* warriors; that the loss of Moscow disrupted the chain of command in the army! To make these rumors more believable, the Field Marshal even publicly quarreled with Cossack Ataman Platov. It was said that he suspected the Cossack of treason and had him removed from the army. Rumors inevitably delivered such pleasant but false news to Napoleon's ears, while Ataman Platov, the genuine son of Russia, gathered young and old in the Don Host and soon returned with forty-five regiments of gallant lads. Napoleon, the great conqueror of Europe, became blinded by his own grandeur, placed himself above the mere mortals and yet fell victim to an ordinary human weakness. A regular general would have seen through such news, but Napoleon believed it because it flattered his expectations. To complete the deception, arrangements were made for the French to intercept our couriers carrying false reports

FROM TARUTINO TO MALOYAROSLAVETS

from the Field Marshal, warning the emperor about disastrous conditions and a lack of fighting spirit in the army. Such reports also claimed that the Field Marshal was unwilling to fight another battle and appealed to His Imperial Majesty to save the fatherland by concluding peace at any cost, on the assumption that the enemy, who was in a difficult situation himself, would moderate his demands. Napoleon, of course, was thrilled to read such intercepted dispatches and was willing to moderate his demands, just wanting to keep the Polish provinces and admitting that he rushed a bit in executing his grand plan of expelling Russians from Europe. But he forgot the *old fox*. Thus, our wise commander prudently played for more time, which played into his hand while driving the enemy into hardship, till cold and hunger reigned and everything was ready to deliver a decisive blow to this terrible foe...

While our troops were retreating through Moscow, one of the first Russian partisans, Colonel [Denis] Davydov of the Akhtyrskii Hussar Regiment, began raiding the main road between Vyazma and Gzhatsk. The Field Marshal later assigned Colonel Davydov, [Alexander] Seslavin, Prince Kudashev and finally Captain Figner to raid the Mozhaisk road. While our main forces rested at the Tarutino camp, our partisans and peasants destroyed enemy foragers and various detachments. This little war spread throughout the territory surrounding Moscow and was conducted with terrible wrath. It caused the French to despair. Our brave partisans, cheering on peasants who had been prepared by the Emperor's appeal and the preaching of the clergy to take vengeance on the enemy, launched a people's war [*narodnaya voina*] in all of its fury and horrors. The Russian people revealed thousands of examples of genuine heroes who fought for the fatherland...

Among our famous partisans, Captain Figner particularly distinguished himself by the extraordinary audacity of his raids. Before I proceed to describing some of his partisan exploits, I must say a few words about his character and early service. Alexander

THE RUSSIAN CAMPAIGN OF 1812

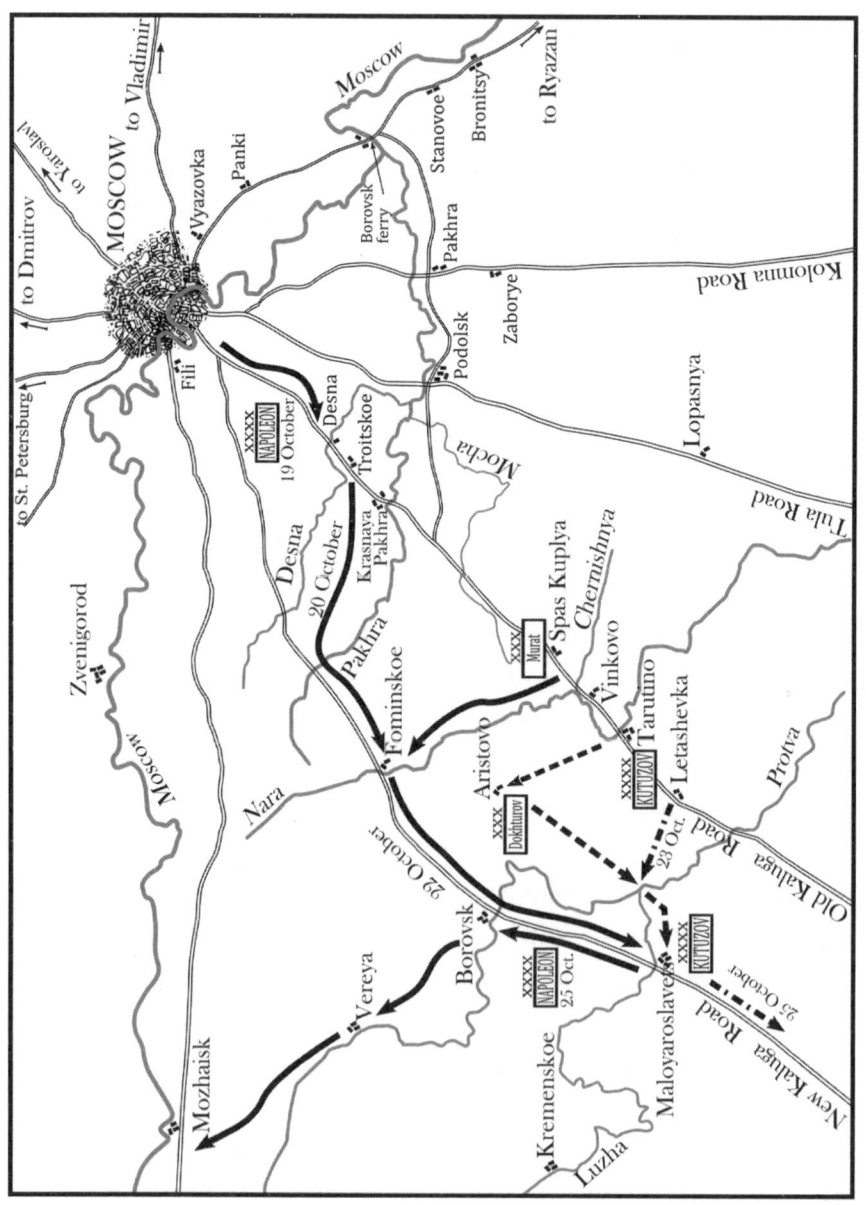

Napoleon's Departure from Moscow.

FROM TARUTINO TO MALOYAROSLAVETS

Samuilovich Figner descended from a noble family of German barons. His grandfather, who migrated from Germany during the reign of Emperor Peter I, had the title of Baron Figner von Ruchmersbah, but it remains unknown which year precisely that he migrated [to Russia,] what [army] branch he served in and how he ended up losing his title of baron. His son, Samuel Figner, began service in the Russian army at the lowest rank and, upon becoming a staff officer, was appointed director of the state crystal manufactury which was located near St. Petersburg. Later, already holding the rank of state councilor and decorated with orders, he retired, but was appointed vice governor of Pskov province. His second son, our partisan Alexander Samuilovich, was born in 1787 and was enrolled in his youth in the artillery corps, where he studied various sciences, revealing rapid progress and excellence, and occasionally demonstrating his extraordinary bravery. At the age of fourteen, he graduated as an artillery officer and was sent to Corfu, where he served under Lieutenant General Borozdin, the local military governor. From Corfu Figner managed to visit Italy and spent several months in Milan. Naturally gifted in everything, he quickly learned the Italian language and spoke it as fluently as native Italians do. Figner often remembered the happy days that he spent in blessed Italy, under a clear sky and temperate climate, amidst abundance of every kind, surrounded by exquisite nature, sciences and arts. He fondly remembered that respectable family in Milan where he lived in a union of love and friendship.

Figner traveled from Italy to Moldavia. In his youth, while still a simple officer, he distinguished himself against the Turks. At Ruse, he measured the fortress moat with the undaunted gallantry of an artillerist and always remained with his gun in the forward trench, on the very glacis of the fortress and showered the Turks with so much canister that they did not dare to appear. At just nineteen years old, he was recognized for his exploits with the rank of lieutenant and decorated with a rather gratifying award, the Order of St. George

4th class, something that rendered this even more flattering being the fact that that the commander-in-chief, General Kamenski, took the cross from the dead body of General Sievers and placed it on Figner's chest as if infusing this young hero with all the courage and intrepidity of the fallen hero.

After receiving such a great reward, Figner rushed to his family in Pskov [in 1811]. Even if the venerable old man died of a stroke a month after his arrival, the arrival of his beloved son after nine years of separation, and with such accomplishments, delighted his father. The death of the father marked the start of a new period in Alexander Figner's life. Staying with his widowed mother in Pskov, he managed, through his good manners and humility, to earn the attention and respect of his father's acquaintances. This soon allowed him to marry Olga Mikhailovna, the daughter of State Councilor Bibikov, who had served as vice governor of Pskov shortly before his father had been appointed.

Due to changes in his personal life, Figner had to travel to the Crimea to transfer the command of his unit. He later transferred to an artillery company that was deployed near St. Petersburg. Returning to his in-laws, he planned to retire from active service to recuperate, but the new war against the French called upon him to return to the field of battle and to seek recognition and glory. He was then assigned as a staff captain to the 3rd Light Company of the 11th Artillery Brigade and joined us in the village of Yashuny, near Vilna, just before military operations commenced.

Alexander Figner was a handsome man, of medium height, a true northerner, strongly built, round-faced, of pale complexion and light hair. His large blue eyes were full of life. He had a spirited voice, sound mind and vivid imagination. He possessed the gift of eloquence and was tireless in action. Contempt for any and all dangers and unmatched gallantry revealed his unwavering intrepidity and presence of mind. He spoke German, French, Italian, Polish and Moldavian as well as he did [his native] Russian. Besides common

FROM TARUTINO TO MALOYAROSLAVETS

facts that any artillery officer had to know, he was well versed in tactics, strategy, ancient and modern history, and read many good books, the only subjects that he admitted to disliking being German metaphysics and mysticism.

And so, Alexander Figner, the man of so many merits, entered the field of glory and became a renowned partisan in Russia and Europe.

After we parted Moscow on September 2 [14], I had no news of him until we were at the Tarutino camp. It was there that he appeared to the great joy of his friends who adored him. We immediately noticed a change in his appearance. He had a beard and his hair was cropped into a circle like that of a Russian peasant. Despite our questioning, and in spite of his good mood because of successful completion of his orders, we could not make him tell us what he did in Moscow. I reminded him of the terrible explosion of the powder magazine that shook the ground. He smiled but looked down and spoke of something else. Humility imposed a seal of certain mystery on his lips. However, given our friendly insistence, Figner slowly revealed to us that, after parting with me, he immediately changed into a Russian peasant's garb and went to Moscow just as the fire began to spread and the French were busy plundering the city. He rallied people of various backgrounds who still remained in Moscow and organized armed detachments to kill enemy soldiers; he ambushed them amidst the flames in the streets and inside homes and commanded his men so efficiently that that the French were killed everywhere, especially at night. And so, accompanied by just a handful of gallant lads, Figner began to kill the enemy inside the city itself, amidst the horrors of burning and plunder. In the flaming ruins of the Russian capital, the French faced a methodical and clandestine war from this courageous avenger, but they searched for him in vain. Even though they had him before their eyes, they still could not find him. In daylight, wearing plain peasant clothes, he walked between French soldiers and served them however he could so he could listen to their conversations. At night, he attacked them with his gallant lads and by morning the streets were covered with the bodies of the killed Frenchmen. Finally, stroking his beard, Figner revealed to us, "I wanted to get inside the Kremlin [to assassinate] Napoleon, but despite my peasant appearance the damn sentry who stood on guard at the Spasskii Gate struck me in the chest violently with the butt of his musket. This raised some suspicion, and I was seized and interrogated on why I wanted to get inside the Kremlin. Though I did my best to pretend to be a fool and simpleton, they kept interrogating and threatening me before releasing me with a warning that I should never ever dare to appear there again, peasants being forbidden to approach the sacred place of the Imperial residence..." After releasing him, the French kept an eye on Figner for some time but he managed to slip away from Moscow, having accomplished what he set out to do.

With his mission successfully completed, our brave and unforgettable avenger returned to the Field Marshal [Kutuzov] at the Tarutino camp. Instead of greeting him, Prince Kutuzov simply kissed him and Figner considered it as the greatest mark of distinction... The Field Marshal instructed him to form a guerrilla detachment and operate, in coordination with other detachments, in the rear of the enemy.

Each partisan was allowed to choose his subordinates based on the weapons that he found most suitable for his task. Figner, who had not earned everyone's trust yet, at first struggled [to find men], but he quickly came up with a new way of finding recruits to set about killing enemy looters. As is well known, on an army's flanks and rear there are always numerous stragglers and foragers scattered around the roads and villages and roads, as well as plenty of layabouts and shirkers. Such men are oftentimes branded as marauders or vagrants, and, by dint of his eloquence, Figner managed to convince some two hundred lads of rather diverse backgrounds to combine their efforts as a means of gaining [greater] booty. Many of them were

FROM TARUTINO TO MALOYAROSLAVETS

light cavalrymen, while the infantry he mounted on peasant nags. At the head of this force, he then launched a series of attacks on the enemy. In daylight, he usually hid them in thickets while, dressed as a Frenchman, a Pole or an Italian, and sometimes with a trumpeter but often alone, personally went to the enemy's outpost where he often reprimanded sentries for their oversight and inattention, telling them that there was a Cossack party in the vicinity. Elsewhere he informed the enemy that the Russians had occupied such-and-such village and it was therefore better to seek forage in the opposite direction. Having reconnoitered the enemy's positions and strength in such a manner, Figner changed into partisan's clothing during the evening and fell like an avalanche with his partisans on the enemy at places where the enemy expected him the least and considered themselves perfectly secure. Operating in such a manner, Figner delivered 200-300 prisoners to the main headquarters on a daily basis, so many, indeed, that it became difficult to accommodate so many of them and he was advised to kill the villains [*zlodei*] on the spot.

With the help of peasants whom he gathered together, armed, and used to collect intelligence on enemy strengths and deployments, Figner was able to constantly reinforce his detachment and even managed to capture an entire enemy battery of six new cannon, together with their caissons, all their equipment and their horses, which had traveled under weak protection from Italy for four months, on the Mozhaisk road. In addition to this prize, he also captured a small chest filled with gold. Distributing this money among his followers, he burned the carriages, wagons and other equipment, and spiked and buried the cannon barrels. Foolish of him though it may have been, however, he took the Italian guards prisoner rather than putting them to death, only for a number of them to manage to flee. Having taken note of Figner's gallantry and talent, one of them, a non-commissioned officer, told the French of his exploits, bravery and cunning alike, the consequence being that Figner's name was soon spreading terror throughout the enemy army and a reward was set for his capture.[1]

To better organize his detachment, Figner set about introducing order and discipline, but the marauders disliked this and ran away. Having demonstrated his ability to cause harm to the enemy even with such limited means, Figner approached Field Marshal [Kutuzov] asking for regular troops and was allowed to select 800 light-cavalry officers and men from amongst the ranks of the hussars, uhlans and cossacks. However, far though he was from ignoring his orders, he had not forgotten about the artillerists, also selecting Lieutenant Sletskii from Lt. Col. Timofeyev's company, and Lieutenant Baron Schlippenbach and Sergeant Kashomin from his own company. I was eager to join him too, but he beseeched me to remain in command of the company that bore his name.

With a detachment of regular troops, Figner became even more dangerous to the French. His military talents only flourished still further, while, through skillful maneuvering, secret marches and swift surprisen attacks guided by local guides on hidden paths, he conducted major raids against the enemy. He routed strong enemy parties, burnt supply transports, intercepted couriers, and harassed the enemy in the whole area round Moscow. Napoleon was even forced to direct infantry and cavalry divisions to put an end to the bold forays of Figner and his partisans on the Mozhaisk road.

---

1 Radozhitskii is clearly reticent to mention a darker side to Figner's character. Many contemporaries attest to Figner's barbarous treatment of the prisoners. In late 1812, K. Biskupskii, who served in his detachment and who overall was of high opinion of Figner, was horrified by his treatment of prisoners. He described how Figner hanged the captured Frenchmen "on pine trees like a ham is hanged to dry out on the sun." Waldemar Löwernstern describes several instances when Figner personally executed defenseless men while another fellow officer (Pavel Grabbe) recalled that "Figner's favorite and most frequent amusement was first to inspire captured officers' trust and cheerfulness by his reassuring conversation, and then suddenly to shoot them with his pistol and watch their agonies before they died. He did this well away from the army, which only heard dark rumors which it either disbelieved or forgot amidst the pressures of military operations."

FROM TARUTINO TO MALOYAROSLAVETS

At one point Figner and his detachment were surrounded on three sides by the French, but he still managed to escape through a clever maneuver. The enemy cavalry wanted to destroy him with his entire detachment and so took time to surround him. Figner sensed the danger and, exploiting the wooded terrain, divided his detachment into two parts. The first was given the appearance of the enemy while the other took a defensive position. The former then appeared out of the woods and pursued the latter, chasing, shooting and fighting them so that the French, who witnessed this action, thought that Figner's detachment was routed and captured. This military trick stopped further enemy action as the French stood by observing the fight and let the daring partisans escape.

On another occasion Figner managed to pull an even more incredible escape. A French detachment ambushed him at a certain spot and pursued him into some woods backed by a swamp. It was already evening and too dark to attempt any operations in wooded terrain, so, fearing that the dangerous partisan would escape, the soldiers surrounded the woods. Convinced, as they were, that the swamp was impassable, it seemed that at dawn they would capture Figner dead or alive. Figner was indeed in a desperate position, for the swamp seemed impassable and was about half a *versta* [600 yards] wide. Nevertheless, under cover of the darkness, he and two of his companions managed to get across the swamp using wooden poles. Coming across a small village, Figner got together a few peasants, and, having explained the danger that hung over his detachment, outlined the plan of action and ordered them to gather hay and wooden boards. Using these materials he laid a wooden path amidst the swamp and returned to his camp where he found his comrades laying behind tree trunks and watching the French as they made merry round their campfires. Gathering them together, he ordered his men to move their horses with great care along the wooden path. This task having been successfully carried out, he instructed his men to form a chain along the path and gradually remove hay and wooden boards as the men passed. As a result, not only was the entire detachment gt away, but the wooden path was disassembled the wooden path without leaving any trace of it. At dawn, the French entered the woods from various sides and combed it to find the partisans. They finally converged at the swamps, wondering where Figner and his Cossacks had gone to. He could not be seen anywhere, nor were there any traces of him. The French cavalrymen tried crossing the swamp on horses but the animals became bogged down and could not move. Figner's trick so astonished the French that they could not quiet down about it for a long time and became convinced that he was not just a terrible brigand who was constantly at their throats, but also some sort of demon. And Figner was, indeed, recklessly audacious, once even attacking Napoleon's guard cuirassiers in their encampment near Moscow and wounding their colonel, who was then taken prisoner together with fifty other men.[2]

At the beginning of the French retreat from Moscow, Figner encountered a large transport train that was laden with plundered property and protected by a strong escort. Lacking sufficient forces to attack it, Figner appealed for help to General Dorokhov, who was nearby with a fairly strong detachment. The general, however, refused to help him for some reason, so Figner contacted another no less famous partisan, [Alexander] Seslavin. Together, they attacked the enemy train and although they could not destroy it completely, they still managed to capture part of it. Figner even sent me a *pud* of some silver which the French had plundered from church icons to decorate the one belonging to our company.

---

[2] Unfortunately, Radozhitskii's account is too vague to determine which unit was involved in this skirmish and where and when. No senior officers of the Imperial Guard were wounded or captured in September-October. In the cuirassier regiments, several captains were wounded in skirmishes near Moscow between September 29 and October 4, but no colonels had been lost during this period. The first cuirassier colonel lost in action was Colonel de Curnieu, of the 12th Cuirassiers, who was severely injured at Orsha on November 21.

FROM TARUTINO TO MALOYAROSLAVETS

Meanwhile, back at the Tarutino camp, our troops had rested and felt as recovered as if they had been billeted in barracks. The soldiers had built sturdy huts and kept them in good shape with brushwood from the surrounding woods. But as mornings turned cold in October and cloudy days announced the approach of the cold winter, officers began building *zemlyanki* [dugouts] and wearing coats [*tulup*]. Fires were constantly maintained at the bivouacs and, as we warmed ourselves around them, we envisioned the miserable fate of the French in our cold climate.

At this time, we received the good news that Count Wittgenstein's corps had scored a victory over Marshal Oudinot and cleared the road from Sebezh to Polotsk, this having also ensured that the routes to St. Petersburg. Shortly thereafter we also heard about General Dorokhov's assault and capture of the town of Vereya which the French had fortified. However, these victories were not celebrated in prayer services as had usually happened before. They seemed to have become ordinary affairs. It was rumored that Napoleon was spreading proclamations to incite the peasants against the landlords in Byelorussia, promising them liberty and freedom from serfdom.

There were also rumors that the position of the enemy army was worsening with each passing day. They had consumed supplies discovered in Moscow and had no other means of procuring new provisions except by feeding on dead horses. Of all the deficiencies that the enemy suffered, the lack of forage was the most palpable. Large detachments of foragers travelled some thirty *verstas* [20 miles] to procure supplies for themselves and their horses and they frequently fell into ambushes that our partisans set up. Thus, each bundle of hay cost them precious blood.

On 23 September [5 October] Count [Jacques Alexandre] Lauriston, Napoleon's aide-de-camp, arrived at the headquarters of our Field Marshal. To receive this envoy, Prince Kutuzov allowed for a few hours armistice to be concluded between the warring vanguards. Meanwhile, orders were issued to move our troops around. Some regiments were redeployed from the camp to beyond the village of Letashevka in order to conceal our actual deployment from the enemy and to give an appearance of our numerical strength by [carefully] arranging the [remaining] troops on open terrain.

Our 4th Corps was then deployed between the vanguard and the main army. We received order to ignite fires in the evening, cook porridge with meat, sing songs and play music everywhere. Thus, the entire camp became illuminated and full of music and merry-making. Our joy was spontaneous upon hearing that Napoleon's envoy would arrive to seek peace from the Field Marshal. It was then that we became certain that we would prevail in this struggle and chase the French out of Russia, so vigorously that they would not get out alive.

It is now well known that the Field Marshal was able to dupe Napoleon through empty conversations and correspondence about peace, while the conqueror of Europe was in desperate need of launching a retreat. Prince Kutuzov, meanwhile, decided to attack [Napoleon's] advance guard which was located on the Cherneshnya River.

During the night of 6 [18] October our troops advanced according to new dispositions for a general attack on the French. The right flank was first to depart in five columns. The 20th Jäger Regiment and ten Cossack regiments under the command of Count Orlov-Denisov opened the march and turned the enemy's left flank. A Guard division of light cavalry moved in support of the Cossacks. It was followed by the 2nd, 3rd, and 4th Corps that comprised the right flank under the command of General Bennigsen. Our troops crossed the Nara River on pre-constructed bridges. The 6th Corps crossed the river in front of Tarutino, while the 7th and 8th Corps moved to the left flank. General Dokhturov's [6th] Corps was followed a large reserve that consisted of the 5th [Guard] Corps, the cuirassiers and the entire reserve artillery. The Cossacks were supposed to deliver a major blow to the enemy's rear, but the Field Marshal apparently expected to face strong resistance which is why he committed his entire army.

FROM TARUTINO TO MALOYAROSLAVETS

The night was not very dark, but the weather was overcast and the ground wet so the troops marched without making a sound; not even the wheels of artillery carriages could be heard. Everyone moved carefully. No one dared to smoke pipes, or strike flints, or cough, and, if anyone had to speak, they all whispered; we even kept horses from neighing. In short, everything became shrouded with secrecy. We thus walked through the night and sleep did not dare to touch our eyelids. Everyone was preoccupied with the pending battle. A glow in the sky soon appeared from the enemy's bivouacs, thereby revealing their location to us. As we marched on so the light shifted until it was well beyond the woods on the left, and, by 4 o'clock in the morning, it was clear that we had successfully flanked the enemy.

Having approaching the woods at the designated spot, the 4th Corps turned to the left and deployed in closed columns with its jagers out in front. We stood there anxiously for some time until the 2nd and 3rd Corps, which had got delayed because of a mistake on the part of their guide, arrived to take up their position on our right flank. The battle began on the right flank at dawn. Just as the sound of gun fire reached us, our jagers charged into the woods and opened a ferocious fire on the closest French troops. I was ordered to move two cannon into the valley to the right of the woods. [As I moved] I saw the jagers of the 2nd Corps running to occupy the woods on my right, the enemy having bivouacked behind these near the burnt-out ruins of the village on the other side of the river. The French were already deployed in line but were visibly in disarray. They had no artillery here, so just a few shots from our cannon were sufficient to spread disorder and force them to fall back. Two French columns, which had been occupying the woods to my left, came out of the forest and began running across the valley to rejoin their brethren. There being no other guns capable of targeting them, I simply fired two solid shots at them and then, having reloaded my cannon with canister, moved closer to them. However, I soon received orders to stop because the infantry protecting us could not keep up. Meanwhile the [French] columns, much to our chagrin, crossed the rivulet and escaped. [By then] the attack had become general while the French, seeing themselves surrounded on all sides, had started to retreat without firing back. They were no longer in columns, but had turned into [disorganized] masses [*tolpa*] that were running away. It seemed to us that if we had started the battle a bit earlier, we could have startled the French while they were sleeping and caught them in their bivouacs: convinced that a peace was in the process of being concluded, they presumed that the lack of activity in the advance guards as confirming the ongoing armistice, which is why they were so unconcerned and careless.

People thought that the root cause as to why our attack was not completely successful lay in the fact that the 2nd Corps, which had the misfortune of losing its corps commander, the gallant General Baggovut, in the very first attack, delayed its further attacks.[3] But Count Orlov-Denisov and his Cossacks delivered a blow to the flank and rear of the enemy. A French light cavalry division stood at the edge of this flank, but could not deploy in time before the Cossacks routed it, losing all of its artillery. Meanwhile, the infantry of the 2nd and 3rd Corps, led by General Bennigsen, with support from cavalry, attacked the enemy so vigorously that disorder spread in the enemy ranks and a rout seemed imminent. Our 4th Corps inadvertently allowed the enemy infantry to escape because lack of cavalry on the one hand and the failure of the 6th Corps to join us on time on the other (something without which it was too dangerous to expose our left flank) meant that we moved very slowly. It seemed that, in launching a general attack over such a wide area, [we] had failed to maintain proper communications and coordination between our units.

---

[3] As bad luck would have it, General Karl Gustav von Baggovut (Baggehufwudt), commanding the 2nd Infantry Corps, was shot dead at very start of the attack, causing confusion among his men and delaying their attack

FROM TARUTINO TO MALOYAROSLAVETS

Meanwhile, General Miloradovich, deployed on the main road across the rivulet to the left of us, charged with his cavalry at the Polish corps and captured Prince Poniatowski's entire train. The 6th Corps and the reserves only moved out of the [Tarutino] camp and did not participate in the battle.

By 10 a.m., our 4th Corps occupied the enemy bivouacs near the village of Dendi. We were startled to see the remains of horses which the French had devoured around their shelters [*balagan*] that were made of various doors, tables, etc. Cooking utensils, pots and kettles were still steaming on fires. We discovered that the French still had some cereal and peas, but lacked bread and beef. We came across a beautiful black colt, with a fine, pebble-grained leather breastplate and bells. Apparently they were fattening him instead of veal.

On this day the enemy was pursued beyond the village of Spas-Kuplya. The cannonade continued for some time until it died down in the distance. As we moved on the main road beyond the village of Dendi, we came across no enemy troops, but did find a spot in the woods where Prince Poniatowski's train had been abandoned. Here we saw several overturned wagons, scattered papers, orders and rosters from the ransacked chancellery. We saw several dead and wounded horses lying in the fields, and occasionally we also encountered dead Frenchmen in worn-out uniforms that were blackened from campfires. In one place we found about thirty sabered Russian jagers and among them several dead French cuirassiers. These were cuirassiers of [Marshal Joachim] Murat, who had attacked the column of the 20th Jaeger Regiment and caused a terrible slaughter.

In the evening, as the gunfire died down, we stopped. Our wounded cavalrymen began returning. One of the uhlans carried a beautiful five-year-old girl in his arms, who was crying inconsolably. He found her in the French supply train, next to her dead mother. This uhlan told us that there were numerous women in the French camp and that among the captured were several beauties from Moscow.

THE RUSSIAN CAMPAIGN OF 1812

After the battle, our entire army fell back to the Tarutino camp, except for the 2nd and 4th Corps which bivouacked near the village of Vinkovo. We considered ourselves victors in this battle and were thrilled to spend the night on the reclaimed ground. With great curiosity, each of us examined all the items that the enemy had abandoned. Seeing how the enemy was feeding on horse flesh, we could not but marvel at their fortitude and devotion to Napoleon.

As darkness fell, Figner rejoined us. He told us that during the attack, he had joined the Cossacks with his detachment and participated in a fierce *melée* against the French cuirassiers; that he got so close to Murat that [the marshal] barely managed to escape wearing only a shirt; that the French had abandoned all their wagons and even caissons; and that their horses could not carry them any longer. So fast were the French running away, indeed, that they were at risk of breaking their necks. After drinking tea with us, Figner returned to his detachment that was in the advance guard.

At night, we were again ordered to light bonfires and sing songs because Murat had sent an envoy through our camp to the Field Marshal [Kutuzov], asking for the heart of his dear friend General [Pierre-César] Dery who had been killed. This alone attests how painful the defeat on the Cherneshnya River must have been for him.

On 9 [21] October General Dorokhov, who was in the town of Borovsk, informed the Field Marshal [Kutuzov] about the appearance of an enemy corps near the village of Fominskoe. He suggested that this corps intended to restore the [French] advance guard's communications with the Smolensk road. The Field Marshal, wishing to determine the enemy's strength, dispatched General Dokhturov's 6th Corps to engage it. Meanwhile, the enterprising partisan Colonel Seslavin, discovered that Napoleon's entire army was in fact moving along the old Kaluga road. He immediately notified General Dokhturov, who was at the village of Aristovo on

FROM TARUTINO TO MALOYAROSLAVETS

his way to Borovsk. The Field Marshal, after learning of Napoleon's intention of moving around the left flank of our army, at once ordered General Dokhturov, together with General Dorokhov's detachment, to proceed to Maloyaroslavets to stop the enemy until all of our forces arrived there. On 12 [24] October General Dokhturov found Maloyaroslavets already in French hands. The entire Russian army departed the Tarutino camp, except for the 2nd and 4th Corps that were assigned to the advance guard under command of General Miloradovich.

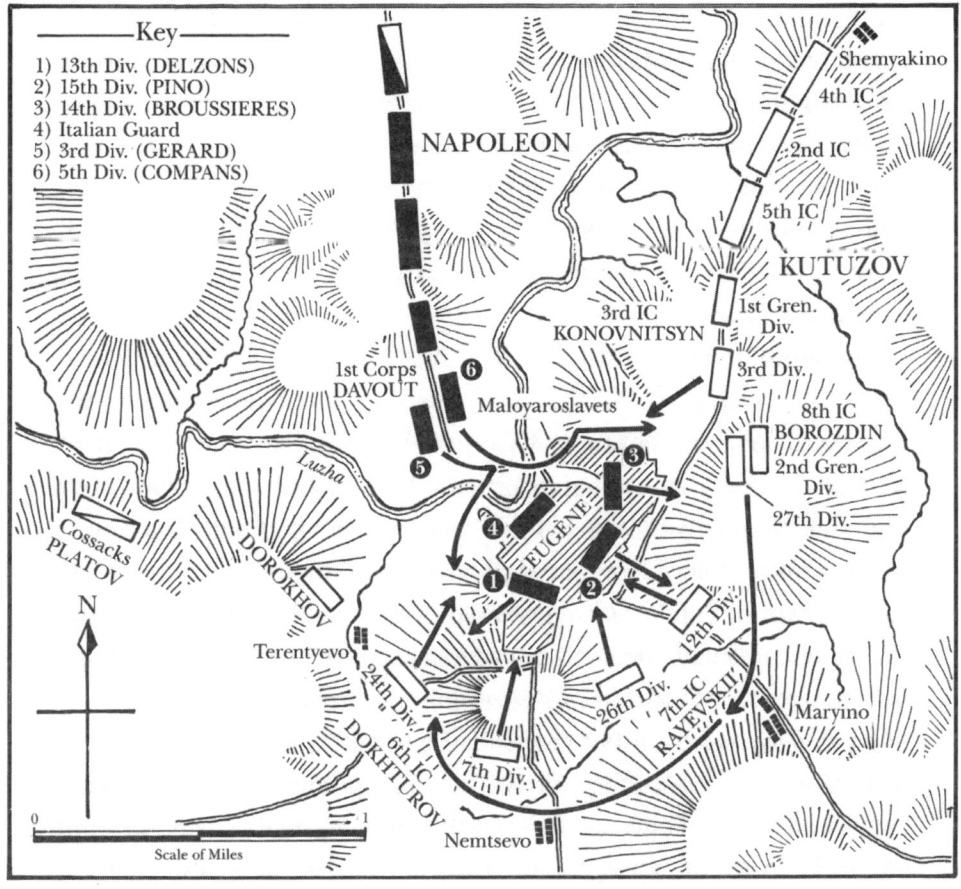

Battle of Maloyaroslavets.

Chapter VIII

From Maloyaroslavets to Vyazma

On 12 [24] October, as the battle raged at Maloyaroslavets and the town changed hands several times, our 4th Corps proved to be the last to arrive on the field of battle; it was already evening. During our march we could hear incessant musket fire and then saw the entire town engulfed in flames. The musket fire continued on both sides until almost midnight. The Cossacks stood behind our skirmisher chain in front of the burning town from where the Italians would regularly charge through the fires like hellish ghouls to engage our skirmishers. In the middle of the night the light of the raging fires illuminated the menacing Russian force and the surrounding heights, revealing a rather stunning sight of the horrors of war. Across the Luzha River, on higher ground beyond the town, the enemy's bivouac fires dotted the area. The 4th Corps and Cossacks spent the entire night under arms in front of the burning town in order to cover the movement of the [Russian] army, which had halted at a new battle position on the Kaluga road about 2.5 *verstas* [1.6 miles] from town.

    The bloody battle of Maloyaroslavets is noteworthy for the incredible determination demonstrated by both sides as well as the ability of General Dokhturov who, together with Dorokhov's detachment, had no more than 10,000 men to defend his position against the 20,000 man strong corps of the Italian Viceroy [Eugene]. If he had allowed the enemy to drive him from this position and open the road to Kaluga, our army would have found itself in rather unfavorable circumstances. But Napoleon himself seems to have hesitated as well. If he had marched with all of his forces to

FROM MALOYAROSLAVETS TO VYAZMA

Maloyaroslavets, he would have accomplished his goal since General Dokhturov's weak corps could not have contained the attack of the whole [French] army.

On 13 [26] October, at dawn of what was an overcast day, we saw the charred and smoldering ruins of the town. We stood at musket range from it, but could not observe a single enemy skirmisher since they were all hiding behind the ruins of houses and fences. The dead silence hanging over the town seemed quite appropriate for the gloomy day and scenes of devastation, and conveyed a sense of ominous terror. We soon received an order to retreat across the stream and join the rest of the army. After spending the entire night under arms, our regiments began to deploy in columns and retreat slowly and in an orderly fashion. The enemy then awoke and fired several shells that burst in the air but caused us no harm. We safely crossed the stream and took position on the right flank of the army, leaving only light cavalry in front of the town.

At Maloyaroslavets Napoleon could see evidence of the terribly hard-fought battle that showed him the remarkable bravery of the Italians and the gallantry of the Russians. From the top of the bell tower, which had survived the fighting, he could observe our army drawn up in battle array. He was certainly surprised that our Field Marshal anticipated his intention of going to Smolensk by a roundabout route. So what was he supposed to do now? He could no longer get to Kaluga except through our army, but this would require fighting a general battle. He could see that the Russian army was strong and ready to oppose him, and could not afford to accept another battle while having no more than 70,000 hungry and exhausted infantry and cavalry. Such a battle would have been lost and ruined his reputation. Thus, this prospect of losing a battle prompted him to start retreating through Borovsk and Vereya toward the main Mozhaisk road and then to Vyazma and Smolensk, hoping to anticipate the Russian army that could proceed by a shorter route through Myadyn and Yuknov to Vyazma and then via Yelnya to Smolensk. The main Mozhaisk road offered scenes of terrible devastation and retreating along this route could only produce great hardship and high losses. However, Napoleon, feeling he was in a desperate situation, decided to take it anyway. He probably exaggerated the necessity of retreating along this devastated route. If he had properly analyzed our intention of defending the Kaluga road, he could have ignored the menacing stance of our army at Maloyaroslavets and ordered his forces to turn from Vereya and the Mozhaisk road to Yukhnov, which was undefended. As a result, he could have led his 70,000 men on a flanking march through the village of Voldakovo and Kremenskoe to Myadyn and then Yukhnov, while containing the attack of our army which would have pursued him at once. Retreating in this direction would not have caused the calamitous disorder and losses which his army experienced soon after embarking on their withdrawal along the Mozhaisk route. From Yukhnov, Napoleon could have blithely marched through Masalsk and Yelnya toward the fertile and untouched regions [of southwestern Russia], with the Russian army close behind him, but with his flanks protected. Thus, the choice of retreating through Borovsk, Mozhaisk and Vyazma seemed inexcusable for a military commander like Napoleon. If he had to choose between two evils, he should have chosen the least of them, yet he opted for the greater one.

The battle of Maloyaroslavets was a turning point that gave our army an upper hand over the enemy. It is therefore rather astonishing that both armies simultaneously began retreating from the town during the night of 14 [26] October. It seemed that each commander-in-chief was perplexed by the other's actions and did not trust their own forces. Napoleon moved his troops to Borovsk, leaving only Davout's corps and a cavalry division at Maloyaroslavets to cover his retreat. Kutuzov also retreated with his entire army to the village of Goncharovo and it was even said that he was ready to fall back beyond the Oka River if Napoleon pursued him. Only an advance guard of two infantry and two cavalry corps, under General Miloradovich, stayed in front of Maloyaroslavets.

FROM MALOYAROSLAVETS TO VYAZMA

During the morning of 14 [26] October, the enemy skirmishers began to engage the Cossacks who slowly retreated. Seeing this, our infantry also broke camp and retreated for some 16 *verstas* [10.5 miles]. We did not expect to avoid another battle and were therefore deployed in battle array in a chosen position. Marshal Davout instead moved away from us in the direction of Borovsk and only left cavalry to watch us.

What followed was the most terrible and unparalleled disaster in military history and, with it, the annihilation of the once so imposing and victorious French army. It had no supplies. Its horses died by the hundreds from lack of forage, or were turned into meals for those whom they had previously carried on their backs. The enemy abandoned [numerous] carriages and transports on the road and blew up caissons due to a lack of horses. An ominous cloud of misfortune hung heavily above the enemy. Starvation, cold, disease, fire and sword all fell upon Napoleon's great army, and death, in terrible forms, descended upon it to claim it victims. Thus, it was that vengeance rose from the ashes of burnt-out Moscow.

On 15 [27] October we continued retreating and took up a new position, marveling that we could neither see enemy behind us nor hear any gunfire. We then received wonderful news that there was not a single French soul [sic!] behind us - they were all gone... We immediately turned around to march forward, reclaiming Maloyaroslavets that evening.

Looking at the charred ruins of houses and churches and the disfigured corpses of those killed, and experiencing the dead silence, emptiness and smoldering stench, it was impossible not to shudder at the horrors born of this ferocious battle. Only the church remained standing in its square, but it was half-burnt near the top while embrasures had been cut in its stone walls and the inside of turned into a citadel by the defenders; it marked the extent of the Russian advance. Behind the church stood a stone gateway with the image of Jesus Christ above the gates. These last drew our attention because their entire surface, from top to bottom, was covered with dents made by the bullets of the Russians as they assailed the church; there was barely an inch of the surface without a bullet mark, and one could barely see the Savior's image above them; the balls, flattened, lay in heaps on the ground. Looking at these balls and the marks on the walls and the gates, one could get a good sense of the ferocity of the Russian musket fire.

The inside of the church offered a rather unpleasant appearance. Our pious soldiers shuddered upon seeing all the impieties that the enemy troops had committed in the holy place: the holy icons - missing their copper frames whose gold or silver-plated appearance had deceived the avaricious robbers - were strewn around on the floor, amidst toppled and smashed statues, ripped vestments, scattered hay, and diverse impurities. The tabernacle doors were smashed, the altar piece damaged, all of the sanctuary utensils shattered and tossed around... But when we approached the sacristy, we were stunned by a new sight – there stood an almost hundred-years old man, gray-haired, beaten and abused; he was the church's sacristan. Remaining true to his duty and not fearing death, he had remained there, amidst all the horrors, firm in his faith in the wisdom of the Almighty. With his voice quivering, he told us how alarm had suddenly spread through the town, how the residents had all run away every which way, and how the enemy had committed numerous cruelties. Some had rushed into the church and began to tear frames from the icons, and, in the process, screaming and cursing, smashed and scattered everything. The old man hid behind the vestments in the closet, but the covetous enemy troops, searching everywhere for plunder, found him there and dragged him out. Some of them threatening him with bayonet and others with sabres, they began to beat and abuse him, asking him, in Russian, where bread and money were hidden. Horror-struck, the old man could not say anything; the enemy soldiers wanted to kill him but a Pole intervened, saying "No need to our sully sabers with the blood of this soulless [*bezdushnyj*] man. Let him live!"

FROM MALOYAROSLAVETS TO VYAZMA

The enemy then heard that the Russian forces were approaching. Alarms sounded in the streets and drums began to beat, and the whole gang of reprobates rushed out of the church. The poor man gathered his last remaining strength and crawled into a remote corner, where he covered himself with pieces of the ripped vestments and, half-alive, kept praying for salvation. Suddenly, another group of ruffians appeared inside the church and spent the entire night punching holes in the church walls. The dawn brought new horrors for the old man: he heard how musket and cannon fire erupted and watched how the church ceiling caught fire threatening to come crushing down and kill everyone inside. The raging flames notwithstanding, the enemy troops kept filling up the church; the crackle of musket fire, fixed with the screams of the fighting men, got worse and worse, but at length it moved away from the church. For a while the old man was left alone with the moaning of the wounded and the sighs of the dying, but then the fighting erupted with new intensity and bullets whistled past his head, and he assured us that Hell itself could not be any worse than what he was forced to witness in those moments. For three days, the old man had eaten not a morsel and the spirit of life was barely holding inside his frail body. Looking at him with deep reverence at him as a true saint and marveling at his survival, our soldiers all gave him whatever they could, be it a coin or a biscuit. Seeing the Russian soldiers, the old man was beside himself from joy, and had clearly gathered his strength to tell everyone about his travails and the horrors of war. I wonder if he survived the war so he could enjoy the universal respect [which he deserved] ... Meanwhile, we rushed across the Luzha River, climbed the steep banks on the far side and stopped for the night at the bivouacs that the enemy had abandoned.

On 16 [28] October General Miloradovich's advance guard marched to Myadyn, while the Yeletskii and Polotskii Regiments, eight of my guns (my other four cannon were attached to Dorokhov's detachment) and the Cossacks remained at Maloyaroslavets. These forces constituted a detachment entrusted to General Karpov to pursue the enemy, but we no longer saw the French, who kept retreating so swiftly that even the Cossacks could not catch up with them.

The following day our detachment joined General Miloradovich's advance guard at the village of Yegorievskoe. We then proceeded to Gzhatsk, spending the night at the village of Golovino. In the villages we passed, we could not find a single peasant there, except for a few old women who would appear amidst the wilderness as ghost-like figures. On the way to the main [Mozhaisk] road, our troops usually set their bivouacs up near the villages as they knew they would provide them with plenty of firewood and straw. It was heart breaking to see how they went to gather them. Fences came down, roofs got dismantled and entire houses disappeared in moments. Then the soldiers, like ants, returned to the camp laden with heavy burdens and built a new village for themselves. Large villages offered shelter for officers as well and my comrades and I occasionally took quarters in a house on the outskirts where, exhausted by the hardships of life in bivouacs, we would lay happily on the straw.

During our marches we sometimes encountered warrior peasants [*voiny-muzhichki*] riding in their carts. One would be holding a long-poled scythe, another a bayonet tied to a club, a third a large nail fixed on a stick to resemble a pike or a pitchfork slung on his back. Very few of them had actual weapons. Riding out of the woods where their entire families were hiding, they welcomed and congratulated us on the flight of the enemy, and assuming a menacing pose, told us of their exploits. We eagerly talked to them and listened to fascinating stories about their experiences during the war.

"At first," one of these warrior-peasants told us, "we were afraid to kill the French in case dragged to court over it. When we occasionally managed to kill a lonely heathen [*nekhrist*], we hid them, damned as they were, in wells or under straw. When at last we heard about the order from the provincial governor, the local *ispravnik* [land captain] told us, 'Lads! Kill Frenchmen whenever you find them!' At this we truly began to fight."

FROM MALOYAROSLAVETS TO VYAZMA

These men were usually led by retired soldiers or Cossacks, but some even elected leaders from among themselves. Upon the enemy's approach to a village, sextons rang all the bells and the armed peasants flocked to the main village square. If the marauders were weak, the peasants attacked and overwhelmed them; otherwise they fled into the woods, where they had moved their wives, children and property in advance. Upon observing French stragglers entering abandoned huts, the men surrounded the building, blocked the doors and, having laid the hay, threatened to burn the huts down unless the French surrendered. One of these peasant-warriors told us, "Three Frenchmen got inside the hut of our elder. So we surrounded them and threatened to set the building on fire. 'Pardon! Take pity on us!' the French began to yell. So our elder took an axe, stood by the door and shouted, 'Alright, we pardon you! Now get out!' But as soon as the first one stuck his head out, the elder struck him with an axe, and the man fell down. A little later, another one tried get out but the elder killed him too. The third one refused to come out for quite some time, even though we threatened to burn him inside the hut. 'Don't be afraid, we will let you off,' we kept telling him. So at long last he decided to come out but not head first, but rather he struck his feet out. But as soon as he did, the elder smashed his feet with an axe and we then strangled him." The peasant-warrior then told us, "Some of our men made such a habit of killing these accursed men that they would buy [the prisoners] from the Cossacks just to have some fun. But, my lord, how would one tolerate what [the French] had done? Just look how they desecrated our sacred cathedrals and sacked our Moscow. Satan himself is inside them, and there is only one way to deal with him."

Another peasant told us about two French cavalrymen who came to his village. These men were tall and strong, wearing full cuirassier outfits, and so the peasants feared being approached by these veritable knights. The giants [*velikany*] entered the hut, and, showing money to the owners, asked them to bring some bread and vodka. The peasants deliberated for a while as to how to get rid of these terrifying guests. They finally decided to let them eat and drink, saying that "once they are full, the [cuirassiers] will certainly take a nap, and we will then be able to kill them." So they gathered vodka, break and milk, and had an old woman delivered them to the [French] warriors [*bogatyri*]. The French were delighted to see it all, and tried to give money to the old woman, but she refused to accept any, fearing that she would be led astray. "And so they began to drink and eat," the peasant told us. "The French kept glancing at us and mumbling something in their language. We pretended to go to our huts but left one chap to keep an eye on them." The story then went as follows: after finishing their meal, one cuirassier took of his cuirass and weapons and laid down on a bench, keeping his unsheathed sword close at hand; the other trooper did not lay down and neither did he undress; he just sat at the table, with a pistol in front of him, and leaning on his hands, rested his head on his fists. They feared the peasants and wanted to take precautions so they could rest in turns. But they were both utterly exhausted and had also eaten a hearty meal, and the result was not only that the cuirassier on the bench quickly fell asleep, but also that the other one began to doze. The peasant lookout let the rest of the village know that the French were asleep. Having been waiting for just this, the peasants gathered in the yard and discussed what to do next. Two of them, one with an axe and the other with a length of rope, volunteered. Taking off their outer clothing, they crossed themselves, and, quietly entering the hut, crawled to the sleeping warriors, and attacked them simultaneously, one of them striking the cuirassier on the bench with an axe, while the other looped the rope around the neck of the cuirassier sitting at the table. The first cuirassier died on the spot, but the other one jumped up and tried to resist, only for the two peasants to each grab an end of the rope and drag him outside before he could do anything. Desperate to avoid being strangled, the Frenchman tried to rush them, but, now joined by many of their fellows, the peasants dodged left and right, still holding the two ends of the rope. In this manner the Frenchman found himself caught in the middle: as soon as he tried to get at one of the groups, the other pulled him back, and for quite some time he was dragged back and forth like a tethered bear. "At last the giant got exhausted and fell down like a rock," the peasant told us. "And then we finished him off with whatever we had at hand." Hearing such stories, it was impossible not to shudder at the resentment the Russian people felt toward their enemies. Their fanaticism oftentimes went far beyond any sense of humanity. So do the rules of war gradually disappear in a people's struggle, and both sides come to act out of a sense of increasing acrimony and destroy one another with all the refinement of barbarism.

On 20 October [1 November] General Miloradovich's advance guard was ten *verstas* [6.6 miles] from Gzatsk. We could see flames devouring the city, which was occupied by the Cossacks. Approaching the Mozhaisk road, we heard exploding caissons and, lined with tall trees, it soon lay in front of us. We saw the French, in thick columns, retreating with great haste. Our soldiers were impatient to attack them. General [Pavel] Choglokov[1] had already shouted to his regiment, "Lads, follow me!" when he was ordered to stop because, already getting dark as it was, nightfall would offer the enemy its protection before our men could engage him. Only General Korff's cavalry had a small fight near Tsarevo-Zaimische. At night we deployed in battle array before setting up our bivouacs. However, realizing that, having spotted our campfires, the enemy might launch a surprise attack, at midnight we changed our location to a new place where we could not be observed as easily. A cold wind with frost portended a fast-approaching winter. Moreover, now that we had reached the route devastated by the French, we had begun to suffer hardship as well. This was especially true for our

---

1 Choglokov commanded the 1st Brigade of the 11th Division of the 4th Corps (after Borodino, he temporarily commanded the entire division) and served as a chef of the Pernovskii Infantry Regiment.

horses: there was no forage available and the poor animals had to be fed rotten straw from roofs. Fortunately I still had a small amount of oats from the Tarutino camp, for, while in charge of Figner's battery, I had gradually built up a reserve which I had used as a treat for our horses. Our experiences worsened with each passing day. The effectiveness of artillery depended on horses and I tried to take good care of them by covering them with horsecloths, while my gunners occasionally fed them some of their biscuits.

The following day the troops advanced parallel to the enemy, about three *verstas* [2 miles] from the main road, remaining idle till the next day. We bivouacked for the night near the village of Spasskoe.

At dawn on 22 October [3 November] we were about twelve *verstas* [8 miles] from Vyazma when we heard gunfire ahead of us. Our advance guard's cavalry soon joined the fighting, while the infantry was ordered to hurry. Everyone ran forward. The infantry formed columns behind the village of Maksimovo, while jagers and my two guns moved forward. General Choglokov ordered us to occupy the forest that was adjacent to the main road. Moving between the skirmishers, I moved forward with two loaded licornes. Our skirmishers entered the woods quietly, without any firing, and stopped just short of the main road. I soon saw French artillery moving on the main road and immediately shouted to the jagers to engage them while firing two shells from my licornes, whereupon I reloaded them with canister and advanced towards the road. Some cossacks, whom a certain Gavrilych had alerted by waving his hat, soon joined me. The French sent their skirmishers against us, and I had to fire canister to beat them back. Red hussars soon appeared behind the enemy skirmishers, but they did not dare to charge upon observing Cossacks behind me.

As I advanced through the brushwood with the skirmishers, the French fell back grudgingly and engaged us in a fierce firefight. We soon reached the main road, where I observed a column of French infantry in gray coats hiding in a ravine beyond the road on the right.

FROM MALOYAROSLAVETS TO VYAZMA

I was concerned that this column would attack our flank, so I halted the jagers and ordered the licornes to prepare to engage the enemy, while I galloped back and brought forward two more of my cannon which I then deployed on the heights on the right. Just as they fired two rounds of solid shot, the entire enemy column ran out of the ravine and into the field, whereupon the Cossacks charged across the road and slaughtered them mercilessly. As I secured the road with jagers and Cossacks, the enemy troops that remained behind us had to turn right and make their way to the town [Vyazma] through the fields. They were pursued by the Yeletskii [Infantry] Regiment under Major Tishin and six cannon of the 2nd Light Company under Lieutenant Dyadin, which I reinforced with two more of my guns, while I myself advanced along the road with the two licornes. While the jagers and Cossacks continued to maintain pressure on the French notwithstanding their intense fire, we came across their supply train. We were greeted with a hail of bullets and cannonballs, but the joint effort of my canister, the jagers' bayonets and the Cossacks' lances disorganized the defenders and we claimed the entire train. During this combat I witnessed a heartrending scene. An old Cossack with a gray beard had been hit in the chest and sat unsteadily on a horse, with his eyes downcast and deathly pallor covering his face. He was supported by two young Cossacks with eyes full of tears, their sorrowful appearance making it all too clear that he was their father. Meanwhile, the rest of their companions were entertaining themselves with the spoils of war. I approached a wagon that had been overturned, scattering numerous books on the ground. No one touched them so they became my bounty. Hastily looking through them, I filled the ammunition chests of both of my licornes' with books. Most of them were medical, but I also found works by Bonnet on botanical flora and physics. Meanwhile, my drummer had found a French skirmisher in the brushwood who, unable to escape anywhere, had quickly surrendered to him. Dragging him along by the collar, he solemnly asked me, "Your honor! What do you want me to do with him?" "Give him to the Cossacks." Releasing the Frenchman, therefore, he shouted "Lads, he is yours!" No sooner had he done so, than several Cossacks rushed at him with lances. Seeing that his death was inevitable, the drummer tried to run away and escape, but was run down and stabbed to death... I reproached myself for the death of this poor soul, but I did not expect the Cossacks to be so embittered as to enact so merciless a vengeance. General Miloradovich soon arrived, praised our actions and, reinforcing us with more infantry and dragoons, ordered us to exert greater pressure on the enemy.

The French corps of the Viceroy [Eugene] still held out in a favorable position on the left side of the road. When we advanced along the road and threatened his left flank and rear, he immediately began retreating toward the town. He was attacked by almost the entire 11th Division and a battalion of the 33rd Jagers. Together with my two licornes, the Cossacks made sure that, so far as the road was concerned, the French did not halt, even for a moment. After my canister shots, the enemy columns became disordered. The jagers charged with bayonets, shouting "Hurrah", while the Cossacks killed those who fled. When a hail of enemy bullets stopped our attack, we repeated the process starting with canister. During this fight I lost one *feuerwerker* and three cannoniers wounded, and two others killed. General Miloradovich, noticing our exploits, sent his adjutant to inquire whose artillery company this was. We replied that it was Figner's and the adjutant wrote down my name and the names of two *feuerwerkers*.

Around noon General Miloradovich dispatched General Paskevich's 26th Division to reinforce the 11th Division. We then advanced en masse and drove the enemy back to the town, where the corps of the Viceroy [Eugene] and Marshal Davout were deployed in strong positions and greeted us with artillery fire. In response, we deployed our own guns in battery, and both sides then maintained an intense cannonade. I was not, however, involved in it because, having been fighting since early morning, my company had run out of ammunition, while the crew was exhausted.

FROM MALOYAROSLAVETS TO VYAZMA

Meanwhile, General Uvarov" cavalry, sent from the main army, struck the enemy's right flank while General Platov and his Cossacks began to turn the French left flank. The French were forced to leave their position and retreat into the town. The columns of the 11th and 26th Divisions pursued them, and, by nightfall, Generals Choglokov and Paskevich had completed their defeat. The former with the Pernovskii Regiment, and the latter with the Belozerskii Regiment, entered the blazing town and cleared its streets with bayonets. Any enemy soldiers who stayed behind in buildings were either killed or captured. The retreating enemy would have suffered even greater losses had not Marshal Ney deployed his corps on the Dorogobuzh road and covered their withdrawal.

This battle pitted much of Napoleon's army against General Miloradovich's advance guard. The boldness with which this disciple of [Generalissimo Alexander] Suvorov attacked the numerically superior enemy forces demonstrated his confidence in the bravery of Russian soldiers motivated by vengeance. The superiority of our arms was becoming clear. The enemy had almost no cavalry and his artillery performed poorly and unsuccessfully.

At nightfall I got my battery together once more, counted the killed and wounded among the crews of the four cannon that had been in action and got it settled down next to the wall of a large stone building that stood at the corner of the street at the entrance [into the town.] Bivouacking here amidst much tomfoolery [*balagan*], we lit fires and cooked porridge. Meanwhile, fires had spread throughout the town while we could occasionally hear explosions and gunfire. We were surrounded by dead and half-dead Frenchmen. Ahead of us constant movement could be heard coming from the road. Because of the blazes raging on all sides and our own campfires, the night was as bright as it usually is during illuminations on great holidays. And quite right too: we really did have a glorious victory to celebrate, and could both clearly see our superiority over the terrible enemy and hope to see him completely destroyed very soon. Officers occasionally approached our fires to warm themselves or drink a cup of tea mixed with stale biscuit, this being the only sustenance that we had to offer them, but the pleasure of driving the enemy out of our fatherland more than made up for any lack of delicacies.

Among the many guests who sat by our bonfire was a musketeer of the Pernovskii Regiment who had been wounded in one hand and was holding a golden epaulette of a staff officer in the other. This soldier told us enthusiastically that his regiment, led by General Choglokov, with banners waving and drums beating, had been the first to charge with bayonets despite a hail of French bullets; that the French, frightened by such a gallant charge, had fled, crushing and trampling each other as they did so; that the men of the Pernovskii Regiment had cleared the street in an instant, killing anyone they encountered; and that the French skirmishers, lodged in houses and firing from their windows, had caused great casualties amongst them, but had been driven out, with half of them killed and the other half captured. During the first attack, the musketeer had stabbed a French colonel with his bayonet and torn off his epaulette, only to stabbed by a French grenadier in turn. At this, he had had to turn back to get bandaged. However, being very proud of his trophy, he had not allowed anyone to take the epaulette away from. How could we have denied such a brave lad a cup of tea for this exploit?

But the most remarkable was a Russian woman, a commoner from Moscow, who was fairly well dressed. She appeared at our bonfire wailing and crying while wrapping a nursing infant in her hands. "Oh, save me, please save me!" she cried. I called to her and, sitting her beside me, consoled her, offering her some tea and asking what had happened to her. She told us that she was hired as [a wet nurse] in Moscow by a married French colonel who had been killed during the battle, and that his wife had been captured by Cossacks outside the town. Managing to escape, she herself had hidden in one of the houses, but, what with the raging fires and all the horrors of war, she no longer knew what to do. Yet she was concerned, not so much for herself, but for the poor orphan baby, whom she constantly fed at her breast, while crying bitterly. "But is he not a Frenchman's son? What do you care?" I asked her. "Oh, if only you knew how kind and gentle these people were! They treated me like one of their relatives. How can I not care for their poor orphan? I will never part with him, only death can separate us!" Although the baby who remained quiet, this kind woman continued to clutch him her body and nurse him, murmuring amidst her tears as she did so "Oh, my poor, poor orphan!" All of us were deeply touched by this incredible sight. Curious soldiers

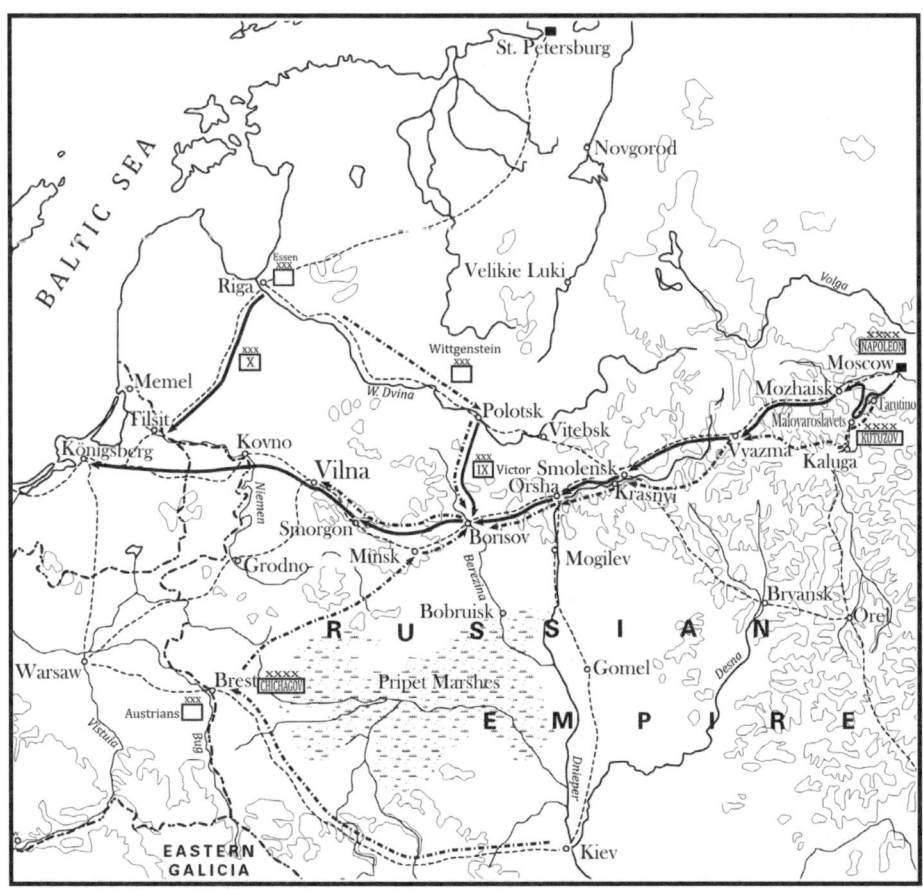

Napoleon's Retreat and the Russian Pursuit.

gathered round the woman who, wanting to hide from the soldiers' prying eyes and having somewhat calmed down, thanked me for the welcome, and then went away to seek a safe haven in which she could take refuge until such time as she could return to Moscow.

The clamour made by the army began to abate little by little, and by midnight the campfires had burned out. Lying under open sky, buried in straw and covered in sheepskin coats and cloaks, we surrendered ourselves to sweet dreams that were yet still impacted by the powerful impressions of the day gone by.

A military career, then, occasionally presents experiences that do not exist in civilian life. The war reveals all of the human horrors and miseries that make our souls tremble, but it also elevates us amidst these dangers. He who has not been to war has not learned how to despise death. The ordinary tribulations of civilian life are nothing compared to the calamities of war, calamities such that neither sighs nor tears can ever change anything. Yet the source of such pity soon runs dry, and the warrior's heart hardens like the steel with which he brings death to the enemy.

Chapter IX

From Vyazma to Krasnyi

Vyazma after the Battle – Signs of Enemy's Hardships – State of Our Forces – Dorogobuzh – Meeting with Figner – Operations of the Observation Corps – Quarters at the Village of Kobyzevo – Field Marshal's Order - Military Observation.

On 23 October [4 November] our advance guard's cavalry continued its pursuit of the enemy while we remained in camp with the infantry. It had snowed during the night and the snow lightly covered the charred ruins of the city and its numerous corpses. The town presented a terrifying sight of devastation. My artillery [company] was ordered to deploy on the other side of town. Moving with my cannon through the streets of Vyazma, I could not look without shuddering at what was transpiring around me. Almost all of the buildings had been destroyed and we were surrounded by their burnt out frames and walls, many of which had collapsed into the streets, blocking our way. The entire town became a mass of rubble and a cemetery. Streets were strewn with corpses of Frenchmen covered with snow; everywhere lay fragments of different weapons, overturned transports, and the charred remains of caissons that had been blown up. We stumbled on cannon occasionally as well. The horrors of this spectacle were augmented by the unbearable stench caused by yesterday's fire. The ruins were still smoldering everywhere. In the middle of the town, we came across a new phenomenon. All the French prisoners were assembled there. There were about two thousands of them, in rags, burnt, blackened, with distorted faces - and what were they doing?

[They were] carving up horse carcasses. Some impatiently cut large chunks of meat; others fervently divided liver and lung, the tenderest parts of the animal. Still others, having claimed the desired parts, happily held them skewered on ramrods and were engaged in noisy conversation. Others roasted their portion at fires ignited next to the ruins, sprinkling their meat with gunpowder instead of salt. Our guards stood around them, watching with disgust at their dealings. They of course recognized the full extent of the [Frenchmen's] distress and felt blessed to still have some biscuits, not being forced to such extremes themselves. Amidst these unfortunate souls, I did not notice any officers. They shared a much better fate since such prisoners were divided into parties that subsequently were sent under Cossack escort further into Russia.

As I passed through Vyazma I by chance encountered Figner, who was passing through with his comrade Colonel Seslavin. He was in such a hurry that he could only spare me a brief greeting. The partisans seemed to be friends. Dressed in a hussar's uniform, Seslavin radiated both audacity and unremitting gallantry. As for Figner, wearing his modest artillery uniform, he was younger than Seslavin but attracted attention with his lively and quirky character. They had both participated in yesterday's battle and their detachments greatly contributed to the fighting against the enemy's right flank.

The following day, we marched in the wake of the French on the main Smolensk road and were horrified to see that the roadway had turned into a continuous cemetery, as if a devastating plague had passed through this region. Every *versta* [0.6 mile] we encountered several dozen corpses of horses and men, with overturned wagons or blown up caissons scattered among them. We saw many frozen horses with their tender parts removed. We even saw, to our amazement, one Frenchman lying inside the horse's gut, holding its liver in his hands, apparently intending to devour it. The severe cold had frozen him in this posture, presenting to us the highest degree of human misery.

FROM VYAZMA TO KRASNYI

Some unfortunate [French] soldiers, who remained on the road, were still alive but so weakened from complete exhaustion and hunger that they lost their ability to communicate and only their slight hand movements indicated that they were still alive. We found a blond officer in this condition, in a thin blue uniform and a three-cornered hat, sitting under a tree next to the road. His eyes were half open, his head bent to one side and a deathly pallor covered his handsome face. He did not respond to our questions, but his right hand moved toward his heart. It was clear that he was about to leave this world. His eyes suddenly froze and he died before us...

Such horrors, which we witnessed throughout our journey after leaving Vyazma, had a profound and uncomfortable impact on us. Even though the French were our enemies and had devastated our homeland, our thirst for revenge could not overshadow our sense of humanity and compassion to such an extent that we could not commiserate with their hardships. Many of our soldiers regarded these horrific scenes with a sense of regret and, being deeply moved by the viciousness of the war, cursed Napoleon as the devourer of the human race, while thanking Providence and their superiors for not having had to experience such misery themselves.

Our troops, meanwhile, were hardly well supplied either. Soldiers lacked biscuits and the porridge that they occasionally cooked was so thin and meagre that one had to struggle to find a single grain in it. At least we were well protected from the cold: back at the Tarutino camp, most of the soldiers in our regiments and batteries had received sheepskin coats [*tulup*] and felt-boots [*valenki*]. In addition, we had since been issued some other warm clothing and still had our ordinary uniforms. As we marched from Vyazma to Dorogobuzh, the winter cold increased and the temperature occasionally plunged to more than 10 degrees of frost.[1] At night we

---

1 Radozhitskii cites temperature in the Réaumur scale, which equals 9.5 degrees Fahrenheit or -12.5 degrees Celsius.

warmed ourselves around bonfires and slept close to the glowing embers, oftentimes burning our sides. During the daytime we were constantly on the move and did not feel as cold. Our horses, however, suffered more from cold and hunger: hay was long gone while oats were soon exhausted as well. We were thrilled when, on encountering old campsites, we found bits of straw and hay to feed our weary horses. At the end of every march after Vyazma, I dispatched foragers with sacks to [search old] cavalry bivouacs to collect whatever remained there. As other regiments were doing the same, my horses became ever more skinny and emaciated, not to mention barely able to draw guns. The loss of men from infantry and artillery alike soon became very noticeable. Despite the fact that we had been almost at full strength at the Tarutino camp, and had not suffered severe losses in any action, the numbers of stragglers and sick had reduced our ranks so much that the entire infantry division, consisting of four regiments, covered a mere half a *versta* [583 yards], while just two or three men marched beside each cannon. Yet, everyone pushed on briskly, oblivious to loss and hardship, and we each march comforted ourselves with the fact that we bivouacked on land reclaimed from the enemy.

Thus we marched with General Miloradovich's advance guard on the devastated road to Dorogobuzh. The main army proceeded along a different route and experienced no hardship.

I will never forget the night of 27 October [8 November] which we spent at Dorogobuzh. We entered the town after nightfall. I deployed cannon by the side of the road and took quarters in the yard of a house on the outskirts of town. There was nothing better to be had, of course, for the houses had all been built of wood and had therefore been burned to the ground, the charred ruins now marking out mere yards, the best of which had been taken over by senior officers. There being nothing that we could use to build bivouacs with either, the soldiers spent the night in great misery in the open air without tents or anything more to warm themselves than campfires. Having done their best to do at those lit by their *artels*[2] bonfires, the men of my battery then lay down to sleep next to horses or under gun-carriages. I [fortunately] had a soldier's tent, which I pitched in a backyard, and shared with my comrade, Lieutenant Baron Ungernsternberg, alone, all the other [company officers] either having gone sick or been sent out on missions of their own.

As we settled down on frozen ground covered with snow and ignited a fire in front of the tent, I looked around and saw numerous corpses of men and horses all around us, dimly lit by the fire. As we had become accustomed to such sights and had more than once enjoyed a sound sleep amidst such a cemetery, forgetting all the prejudices of childhood, we paid no attention to them this time and tried to warm our stiffened limbs. Meanwhile, the light of the fire and sight of the tent, which was set up away from the others, attracted wounded and exhausted Frenchmen, who came lurching out of the ruins like ghosts. The first to approach us was a tall and skinny German, probably a cavalryman though we could not discern any uniform on him. We noticed that his legs, for want of shoes, were wrapped in sacking that the wily fellow had bound up as far as his knees. His face was as black as his clothing, his head wrapped in rags, his hands not visible as they clung tightly to his body, and in general looking like a scarecrow. The first words he uttered in a weak, suffering voice were "Erbarmet euch, gebt mir Brot! [For the sake of compassion, give me some bread!] He sat down beside the fire. His contorted face took on a joyful appearance from the wholesome warmth of the fire, especially after we gave him a dry biscuit soaked in hot water. He fervently gnawed on it, continually thanking us. We asked him about Napoleon, and, no sooner had the name been uttered, a stream of curses burst from the poor man's lips. "Sey er verdammt und verflucht in Ewigkeit!"

---

2 Artel was a soldiers' corporation, usually eight to ten men pooling their resources and money to help each other survive army life and campaigns

[Cursed and damned be he for eternity!], he cried Soon after him came another one, a true Frenchman in a greatcoat and shako, who walked propped on a crutch thanks to a wounded leg. He seemed to be more cheerful, though also very fatigued and weak. His first word was, "Messieurs! du pain!" [Gentlemen! Some bread!] Then the tall German stopped cursing Napoleon and probably out of his hatred for the French, he stood up, thanked us and went to look for another refuge. The Frenchman spoke sporadically, and, when he did so, only complained about the cold. Having already drunk tea, we gave him a dry biscuit [i.e. not soaked in water] but he was unable to chew it. Seeing the Frenchman's futile efforts, I asked him if he would consider eating horse meat. "Why not?" he said. "There are no limits when it comes to hardship!" So I pointed to a nearby horse and suggested that he might be able to satisfy his hunger at once. "If only I had something to cut the flesh with," he wondered [out loud]. We gave him an axe. I wanted to see what he would do. The Frenchman, with axe in hand, doddered toward the horse and, dropping to his knees, began to strike it with all the might that he still had. But the corpse had been petrified from cold. Seeing that it was impossible for him to get meat, the poor man returned to the fire, and laying down the axe, he said very calmly, "Que faire! Il faut mourir!" [What else to do! There is nothing for it but to die!], and lay down on the ground. His words made a strong impression on me. I was awed by his remarkable fortitude in the face of merciless reality and the indifference with which he expected death! He uttered not the slightest cry or wail, not the slightest complaint against the person behind of all his sufferings [Napoleon]! Deeply touched by his hardship, I offered him whatever biscuits I still had, but the Frenchman refused to take them, saying that he could not abuse my generosity... At length, the fire burned down, whereupon the extreme cold soon forced me to leave the Frenchman to his dreadful fate and sink into a marmot-like hibernation inside my tent covered by my sheepskin coat.

FROM VYAZMA TO KRASNYI

On 27 October [8 November], General Miloradovich's advance guard turned left and proceeded along country roads, leaving pursuit of the enemy on the main road to General Yurkovskii's Cossacks and dragoons.

As we approached Lyakhov, we encountered French prisoners from the routed brigade of General [Jean] Augereau.[3] Of all the enemy units, this was the only one that surrendered to Russians almost without a fight and did not experience any of those calamities that befell the rest of the army. The prisoners seemed to be well fed, in new blue uniforms with yellow facings. Many of them were without boots, and shod in no more than shoes and leggings, and the men concerned complained bitterly about the Cossacks, who plundered them. In front of the village, we came across several troopers who had resisted our guerrillas and been dismembered. Severed hands lay next to their stripped corpses and the helmets bound with tiger's skin indicated that they had been either dragoons or cuirassiers.

I was particularly delighted to see Captain Figner, who was escorting a crowd of some 2,000 prisoners. In a few words he told me that these fat [*otkormlenyi*] cowards had surrendered, almost without a shot, at the first appearance of Cossacks. It seemed unusual to see Figner escorting prisoners away from the theater of operations, but he told us that he had the Field Marshal's order to deliver reports to the Emperor in St. Petersburg. With this mission, the Field Marshal wanted to reward Figner for his great exploits, and the glorious partisan duly had the good fortune of enjoying the Emperor's grace. Thus, upon arriving in St. Petersburg, he was promoted to lieutenant colonel and transferred to the artillery of the Guard, while his father-in-law was forgiven a debt of 30,000 rubles that he owed to the treasury.

---

3 Jean Pierre Augereau, the brother of Marshal Charles Pierre Augereau, commanded the 1st Brigade of the 1st Reserve Division and was forced to surrender near Lyakhov on 9 November. He spent a year and a half in Russian captivity and returned to France in August 1814.

THE RUSSIAN CAMPAIGN OF 1812

On 30 October [11 November], our 4th Corps joined the main army and together with the 8th Infantry Corps and 2nd Cavalry Corps, it comprised a corps of observation under the command of Count Osterman-Tolstoy. The following day this corps of observation moved to the village of Luchinki and, forming the main army's rear guard, proceeded toward the town of Krasnyi. On 1 [13] November, the 11th Division, in which I served alongside my artillery, entered the village of Chervonnaya. The following day it arrived at Kobyzevo.

When on the 4th [16 November], Italian Viceroy [Eugene's] corps was defeated upon retreating from Smolensk, thanks to Captain Semchevskii of the Pernovskii Infantry Regiment, who had been dispatched with a company to the nearest woods, the division picked up some scattered French soldiers at no more cost than a few musket shots. By now, our infantry companies rarely exceeded 80 men, and some regiments only had 300-500 men present. An entire infantry brigade seemed like a battalion and an entire division a regiment. It was probably for this reason that our 4th Corps was removed from the advance guard and, by extension, why we did not participate in the defeats of the corps of Viceroy [Eugene] and Marshals Davout and Ney, but simply rounded up their vanquished and scattered remnants. Thus, in three days, the 4th Corps gathered some 4,000 prisoners without any fighting. This circumstance is quite remarkable in the annals of military history and attests to the vision of the Field Marshal. The prisoners – exhausted and blackened, with bandaged ears and heads and wearing ragged overcoats, torn shakos and hideous shoes,– represented the pitiful remnants of the once terrible army of the conqueror of Europe. They were extremely frightened of the Cossacks, who constantly harassed them day and night.

Meanwhile, changes were made in our corps' artillery. Captain Figner, who had distinguished himself through partisan raids and had been sent to St. Petersburg, was transferred to the Guard. The third artillery company, which wore his name, was placed under command of Lieutenant Colonel Timofeyev while I, despite actually commanding the company during the Patriotic War, was still kept as a senior officer.

We spent several days quartered at the village of Kobyzevo, occupying warm houses, some of which were still occupied by the remaining peasants. They told us stories about the French, whom they found rather miserable: staggering from house to house, without weapons and looking like beggars, Napoleon's soldiers pleaded for a piece of bread with which to prolong their sorrowful existence. At least here they were not slaughtered as ruthlessly as near Moscow. The owner of the house where we quartered told me that prior to the Russian army's arrival, a French colonel and three officers (one of whom spoke Russian) quartered at this house. "You should have seen how humble and meek they were," he said, "as they begged me for bread and other provisions, giving me all the money they had and beseeching me to spare their lives. It was impossible not to take pity on them: they seemed so docile, kind, and destitute that it was impossible for me, however reluctantly, not to share what God has given me with them. These poor fellows assured me that it was Bonaparte, not them, who should be blamed for misfortunes that befell Russia; it was him who led them where they had no wish to go. "What do we have to gain in Russia?" they said. What is here that we have not seen elsewhere"… Such stories suggested that in the lands around Smolensk, the peasants had not been excessively despoiled by the French, and therefore did not feel as embittered toward them and commit so many horrific acts of vengeance against them as the residents of other towns and villages that had been devastated around Moscow, Mozhaisk and Vyazma.

How much the French feared a Russian peasant can be judged from the following example. Lt. Col. Timofeyev, our new commander, took up quarters separately in a peasant hut [*izba*] that, if very small, was also very warm, where we gathered every day to drink tea and talk. The hut, as expected, featured a huge [traditional Russian] stove with *podpechek*.⁴ People soon noticed that bread crusts and pieces of meat left on the table disappeared overnight, even though the house was locked from inside. The batman, who slept by the door, assured everyone that he did nothing during the night except for sleeping like a log. Once, as we gathered as usual at the Lieutenant Colonel's house, we joked that it was probably the ghosts of starved Frenchmen, who were getting their way into the house through chinks in the logs at night and eating what they so desperately sought in the last moments of their earthly existence. It so happened that, at that moment one of the officers, standing next to the burning stove, decided to smoke his pipe. He, however, dropped a piece of paper and as he bent down to pick it up, he noticed something moving under the stove. The batman was quickly summoned and to everyone's surprise he pulled a pale and exhausted Frenchman, wearing ragged cloths, out from underneath. He was scared to death and, upon emerging, fell to his knees and begged for mercy in a trembling voice with tears in his eyes. We laughed, feeling sorry for him. Seeing our compassion, the Frenchman calmed down and admitted that hunger made him leave his shelter to steal food at night, whilst he also claimed that, after spending a week in this hole, he had got quite used to it. He slept during the daytime and looked for anything edible at night; at times taking advantage of darkness and the deep slumber of our men, he even quietly opened the door and went out to catch some fresh air. Frightened of the Russian soldiers and dreading the revenge of the Russian peasants, he had secretly made his way into this empty house and found shelter in this warm spot [under the stove.] This new Diogenes was immediately sent to the duty officers [*dezhurstvo*] and later joined his comrades, to whom he could certainly tell many stories about his warm quarters. Without a doubt the many poor souls like him had plenty of stories of such strange incidents to swap,

---

4 Podpecheck - a space under the stove for storing cooking utensils.

always provided that, suffering from cold and hunger as they were, they could still move their tongues.

We soon received the order from the Field Marshal announcing a brilliant victory of General [Matvei] Platov over an enemy corps marching from Dorogobuzh to Dukhovshchina. Among other things, the order stated, "With the extraordinary successes that we celebrate every day and everywhere over the enemy, we now need only to pursue him speedily. Then, perhaps, the Russian soil, which the enemy dreamed of enslaving, will be covered with his bones. Therefore, we will pursue relentlessly. Winter is coming, and with it, blizzards and cold. But you, the children of the North, have nothing to fear! Neither extreme weather nor the enemy's stubbornness can harm the iron chests that represent the impregnable walls of our homeland. May everyone remember [Generalissimo Alexander] Suvorov, who taught us to endure hunger and cold to achieve a victory, for the sake of glory for the Russian people. Forward! The Lord is with us! A shattered enemy is in front of us! May peace and tranquility reign behind us!"

This order had an effect on us; officers and soldiers cheerfully repeated, "We are the children of the North! We have chests of iron and fists of solid rock! We do not fear the cold! Forward, let's finish off the French!" This shows how important it is for a military commander to have an eloquent orator serving him unless, better still, he himself can pour out his heroic feelings in expressive terms! His words, like heavenly manna, inspired the spirits of soldiers: growing weaker from exhaustion though they might have been, they were yet enlivened by the courage of their leader. Hence the many miraculous feats that they wrought that are inexplicable to ordinary people.

Prince Kutuzov's actions demonstrated his wisdom, deep knowledge of military art, and a sense of prudence, all of which was confirmed further by his continued successes. Therefore, no one held him responsible for not delivering a decisive blow to the

THE RUSSIAN CAMPAIGN OF 1812

enemy at Krasnyi even though he had equal number of men and a clear superiority in cannon. It is probable that our Field Marshal did not believe Napoleon's army to be in complete disorder, in which it actually was upon departing from Smolensk, as we have learned since then. On the contrary, in the first battle at Krasnyi the French demonstrated remarkable determination, resilience, and incredible gallantry. Their resistance would only have intensified if they were pushed to the brink of destruction without any hope of salvation. Thus, fighting to the last and dying with weapons in hand, they would have shed the blood of many Russian soldiers, the lives of every one of which were precious given the prospect of a prolonged struggle aimed at finishing what had been started so successfully. The Field Marshal, of course, did not want to gamble the fate of the fatherland in a decisive battle. Our troops were not in an enviable position, and they had also endured hardship, though not as extreme as that experienced by the enemy. Still, they had suffered considerable losses as an exhausting campaign and scanty provisions rendered more and more men tired and sick. Only love for their homeland and the growing sense that they had triumphed over the enemy kept their spirits motivated. By avoiding a general engagement at Krasnyi, our army avoided significant losses and consequently retained that formidable and imposing appearance with which it entered Germany, and swayed the European courts in favor of Russia. Pondering these future circumstances, the Field Marshal showed no intention of undertaking any major effort to complete the destruction of Napoleon's army. It seems that, out of love for Russia, he chose not to seek this glory. The skill with which he managed to bring the army of the great conqueror, who had spread terror in all of Europe, to such an extreme condition is in itself a remarkable accomplishment. It must be noted that all of Field Marshal Prince Kutuzov's military operations from Moscow to Krasnyi were carried out with a high level of strategic consideration, far superior to all other military operations that our armies had carried out up to that moment.

FROM VYAZMA TO KRASNYI

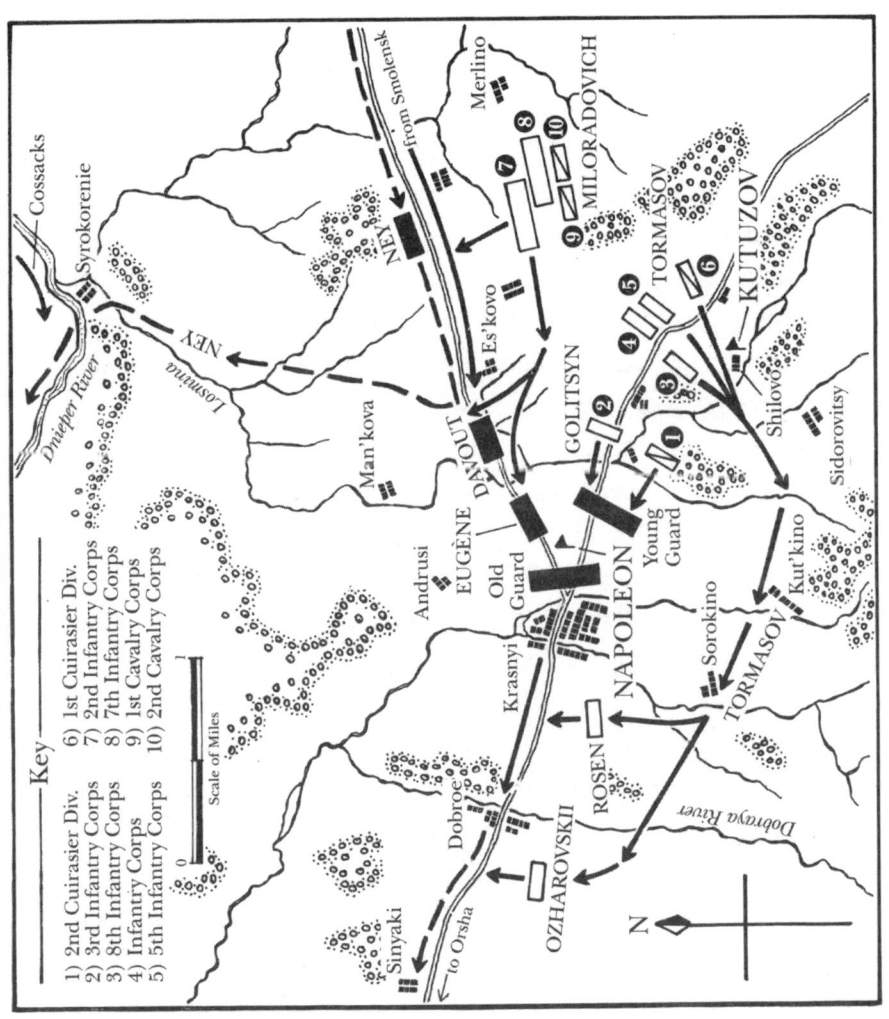

Battle of Krasnyi.

Chapter X

From Krasnyi to Grodno

From Krasnyi, the army of Field Marshal Prince Kutuzov advanced slowly, moving by short marches while quartering in villages that were less devastated. The 4th Corps of Osterman-Tolstoy moved in a separate column; both of its divisions counted no more than 3,000 men with just 18 guns. If other corps were equally small, our army, upon approaching the Berezina, was indeed weakened; but it seems some regiments and artillery companies were left at depots for reorganization.

The advance guard, under the command of General Miloradovich, crossed the Dnieper River at Kopys on 11 [23] November. We arrived there in its wake on the 12th [24 November] and rested for a day. Arriving at a village that had been plundered but not utterly devastated, it was here that, for the first time after a five month long retreat and then pursuit, we saw some Jews [*zhidy*]. Despite the hideous appearance of these swindlers [*obmanshiki*], we were pretty happy to find fellow human beings living in warm homes with their families; scarce though food had been in the countryside as a whole, they had yet been able to feed themselves, and even offer to sell we soldiers, who had nothing but biscuit, some supplies. At first, only old women appeared, but, then, upon seeing that we had money and meant no harm, men started to come out as well. We treated them well and they told us about both the suffering they had endured at the hands of the French and the manner in which they had been forced to please them. "But we did know," one of the Jews told us, "that they would end up badly because our Sovereign had both the might of his army and the might of his people behind him. And so it came to pass. When we heard that the French had captured and burned Moscow, we became frightened and the rabbis imposed a fast on all the Jews! For twelve days, we stayed inside and ate and drank nothing, but kept praying to the Lord to return the Muscovites [*Moskali*]. And so it came to pass. May the Lord help you and us. The French are fleeing and will never come back." Another Jew admitted that the French often dispatched some Jews as spies into our army and paid them in gold. "Yet no-one actually wanted to take their filthy pennies!" said the Jew, frowning. "There were also some who went to the Muscovite army and informed their generals about what was happening among the French, without asking any payment for it." All this said, the Jews and their homes had survived both [Russians and the French], while the Russians had seen their homes burned or torn to pieces for bivouacs, and they themselves driven into the woods and forced to suffer agonies from hunger and cold.

In Kopys, our army received various supplies from mobile stores. We received pay, fresh biscuit, oats for the horses and other provisions; we also stocked up on sugar, tea, vodka and all sorts of others things that could be had from either our sutlers and or the Jews. Thus, thanks to the wise orders of the Field Marshal, the troops were rejuvenated and each of us, thrilled to satisfy our basic needs, thanked him from the bottom of our hearts for his care.

In Kopys, the Field Marshal gave orders for the cannon of twelve artillery companies to be left behind, and reassigned their crews and horses to active field units. Either because it was Figner's or - maybe - because of the great challenges it had overcome while serving in the advance guard, our company was among those that was kept with the army and received men and horses. Needless to say, I was rather pleased to remain on active duty.

On 14 [26] November we departed from Kopys and continued to advance parallel to the road that the French had taken; General Yermolov, leading a special detachment, was tasked with pursuing the enemy. The artillery of the 4th Corps, consisting of just 18 guns under command of Lt. Col. Timofeyev, moved separately from the infantry, which occupied entire villages for quarters. We could not find local residents anywhere and the settlements were all abandoned; as the expression goes, one could neither find cats or dogs. Barns and sheds were all cleaned out: not a single grain of corn, grain or a tuft of hay could be found. All this said, at least the peasants' houses were still standing, the result being that there was plenty of straw which we could use to keep warm and even feed to our horses.

The winter had not turned harsh yet. We passed through vast pine forests that sheltered us from cold. At last, we crossed the Berezina River on a wooden bridge that was fastened with ropes to the riverbanks; these last, meanwhile, were flat and covered with woods, while, thanks to all the snow the muddy water was very deep and flowed with great rapidity. The river was no more than 30 *sazhens* [210 feet] wide, and it had consumed several thousands of the fugitives who had once claimed to be the conquerors of Russia.

Even before crossing the Dnieper at Kopys, we learned about the victories of Count Wittgenstein, who had taken Polotsk by assault, and then pushed Marshal [Charles Nicholas] Oudinot's [2nd] Corps back to the Berezina. We also learned that General [Faddei] Steinheil had defeated the Bavarians, capturing their treasure chest and flags. As we pondered these victories and those of our main army, we were certain that the Field Marshal had not promised in vain that he would cover Russia's soil with the enemy's skeletons. Now, as we approached Minsk, we learned with great pleasure how easily we had captured not only the town but also all of its military depots and supply magazines.[1] However,

---

1 The town of Minsk held an important place in the French line of communication and Napoleon himself described it as "the grand depot of the army". Governed by Polish General Mikolai (Nicolas) Bronikowski since July, the city was protected by a small garrison of some 2,200 men, supported by General Ksawery Kossecki's Lithuanian troops (some 3,500 men). Aware of Chichagov's advance from Nesvizh, General Bronikowski failed to rise to the occasion and chose to engage the Russians by sending out a portion of his troops (under Kossecki) to defend the crossing over the Nieman at Novy-Sverzhen. The Russian advance guard routed Kossecki at Novy-Sverzhen and Kaidanov on 14–15 November, capturing the crossings intact. Bronikowski then promptly abandoned Minsk and withdrew to Borisov. On 16 November, the Russians entered Minsk, capturing large quantities of supplies the Poles left intact, including hundreds of thousands of rations, over 2,500 muskets and plenty of ammunition.

FROM KRASNYI TO GRODNO

we had to pass bypass the place because it housed a considerable number of sick and wounded.[2]

Rumors had claimed that Admiral [Paul] Chichagov's army had moved into position to prevent the French from escaping over the Berezina, and we had therefore looked forward to seeing Napoleon himself in our hands. One can imagine how disappointed we all were to learn that [Napoleon] had managed to break through with part of his forces by concealing his crossing site from the Admiral.[3] It was said that then river ended up choked so many wagons and corpses that they came to form a bridge of sorts. Never before had such a terrible crossing occurred in military history. It was said that our Field Marshal was deeply saddened to receive the news of Napoleon's army breaking through [Chichagov's defenses] and, leaving the main army to General Tormasov at Ush, he went in person to the Admiral's army which was pursuing the French.

When we reached the main road from Minsk to Vilna, which our unfortunate enemy used to escape, we encountered numerous overturned wagons, corpses of killed or frozen humans and horses, scattered on and under snow over which our artillery had to move. On one occasion my cannon got stuck in a pothole and almost turned over. I rushed with my cannoniers to hold it up and was shocked to see that the wheel was, in fact, stuck in between the bones of a frozen corpse that was covered by snow. We oftentimes saw two or three blackened and frost-bitten Frenchmen, some still carrying their muskets, stumbling around like phantoms in a snowdrift alongside the road, but no one paid any attention to them. Once we met two Russian women, who, with clubs in hand, were escorting about three dozen ragged and half-frozen Frenchmen. Upon seeing the jubilation

---

2 When the Russians entered Minsk, they captured hundreds of Allied soldiers (Admiral Paul Chichagov reported 2,224 men but French officer Vaudancourt claimed as many as 4,700 men) convalescing in local hospitals, and liberated 110 Russian prisoners of war. In his letter to Emperor Alexander, Chichagov described the dreadful conditions in hospitals and the town in general.

3 The Grande Armée crossed the Berezina between 26 and 29 November.

THE RUSSIAN CAMPAIGN OF 1812

of these women as they led their captive enemies, we could not but laugh, but on the other hand, we could not but feel sorry upon seeing how humiliated and disgraced these once proud conquerors of Europe had become. We often came across stragglers who were bundled up in rags and huddled like ugly stuffed scarecrows as they fled toward Vilna. Seeing our officers, they would beseech us in a weak voice, "Monsieur! Du pain [some bread]!" and when no one paid attention to them, they emitted a heavy sigh, crying out, "Oh, mon Dieu! Mon Dieu!" We were particularly struck by the sight of one of these unfortunates. Like the others, he could barely move his legs, but what legs these were! Completely naked and with straw frozen to them, his legs were blackened by mud and covered with an icy crust, beneath which we could see that his toes were wrapped in straw. His feet were frost-bitten to the knees but somehow this unfortunate man managed to draw near and even ask us for some bread. Our soldiers stopped to look at him and, shuddering at his misery, gave him a little biscuit.

Along the way we occasionally stopped at taverns and were usually treated to terrible sights inside. Ordinarily, there was a fire in the middle of the room and frozen Frenchmen lay all around it on the floor; those closest to the fire were still moving but the rest were all dead, their bodies distorted and faces disfigured. Such were the calamities that befell Napoleon'ss great army…

At the end of November[4] we began to suffer from the extreme harshness of winter. Our soldiers also became blackened [by frostbite] and wrapped in rags; some wore half-coats or sheepskin coats, *kenga*[5] or felt boots [*valenki*], and fur hats so that when they put down their arms, they no longer looked like soldiers. Officers were not better dressed. I myself barely survived that winter wearing a sheepskin coat and double felt boots while my head was wrapped in a large scarf. The clothing was so heavy that we could not walk for long, and yet

---

4 Early December under Gregorian calendar.

5 From Finnish kenka, these were special winter covers, lined with fur and put on boots.

the severe frost also prevented us from sitting. Our artillery lieutenant colonel always travelled in a sleigh ahead of us, wrapped in a bearskin coat; a duty officer was always required to follow our company from behind, while the remaining officers moved in the front and could use the lieutenant colonel's sled. But whoever decided to sit down had to jump out very soon and run a few miles to warm himself up; on such occasions, we were treated to the precious keg of Kizlyar vodka, which the lieutenant colonel kept between his legs inside a sled. Not being a drinker and in fact having never tasted a glass of vodka, I drank two full glasses of vodka without any snacks every day, so that, if I entered a warm room at the end of a march, I felt a burning sensation, while my head was spun so much that I could barely stand on my feet. In such conditions many officers and soldiers became severely ill or suffered frostbite; almost everyone had some part of his body frost-bitten and, in my case, it was my heels. Enduring such hardship, we could not but marvel how the French, who were deprived of any means of subsistence and protection from the elements, managed to survive. Indeed, it should be considered a miracle that a few hundred despondent soldiers managed to endure calamities that were unprecedented in military history, one may even say unbelievable disasters, during their flight from Moscow to the [Russian] borders...

Our horses had also suffered extreme deprivation because they had no hay and, apart from occasional scanty portions of oats about the size of a handful, they had to feed on straw. All the villages were deserted. Having earlier sided with the French, the Poles now feared Russian retribution. Our artillery moved very slowly and, thanks to the constant attrition in terms of men and horses, could hardly act against the enemy. Our horses had to be frequently re-shoed, while, every time we came to a hill, even a minor one, we had a real struggle struggle to get up it: we had to harness a second set of horses, and force them to drag the cannon up by means of violent shouts and many a crack of the whip. We had to abandon many of our horses dead along the road. Thus, even for us, the children of the North with the iron chests [as Kutuzov put it], this pursuit proved to be filled with enormous challenges, hardships and losses.

Field Marshal Prince Kutuzov's main army slowly approached Vilna, moving in the wake of Admiral Chichagov's troops. In early December we arrived at Bogdanovo, where we rested at warm quarters for one week, and, on 8 [20] December, Oshmyany, where we came across the same signs of the fleeing enemy: numerous corpses, and scattered cannons and caissons. It was said that an entire division of Italians had been destroyed here by the partisan Seslavin. Not far from the main road there was a large pile of hundreds of naked bodies covered with snow. This was the last image of disasters that had befallen the enemy: deformed torsos, twisted faces, clenched fists, grinning teeth, eyes that were bulging and glassy: everything testified to the terrible suffering and despair of the victims. Their bodies were piled one upon another as if they were frozen while struggling with death: one was sitting, baring his teeth; another was standing with a raised fist, and still another, with arms outstretched, staring at us with his bolting from his head. Meanwhile, others again were lying on their back with their feet in the air or even standing upside down on their heads... From a distance, this pile of naked corpses in the snow represented something completely extraordinary and attracted the curious among us. But the sight of human bodies, turned into distorted statues by the fierce frost, caused every one of us to shudder and depart in horror.

On 10 [22] December our artillery stopped at the village of Paradomino, about fifteen *verstas* [10 miles] from Vilna. Meanwhile, as the forces of Admiral Chichagov and Count Wittgenstein as well other flying detachments drove the enemy out of Russia and pursued his survivors all the way to the Vistula, the main army of the Field Marshal [Kutuzov] took up winter quarters around Vilna, Oshmyany and Wilkomir. That day our Emperor deigned to come to Vilna. Rumors claimed that the Field Marshal organized a brilliant reception for His Majesty and threw trophies taken from the enemy at the feet of our monarch: numerous eagles, banners, etc. The city had been cleared of corpses, and beautifully illuminated; it seemed as if all human suffering disappeared at the presence of the benevolent Sovereign. Despite the duplicity of the Lithuanian [Polish] nobility and people, the Emperor deigned to graciously accept their delegates and on 12 [24] December, he issued a memorable manifesto forgiving them and calling on the populace to return to their homes and, in recognition of the kindness of thire legitimate monarch, repent the momentary blunder of allowing Napoleon to seduce them. Field Marshal Kutuzov, Prince of Smolensk, was awarded the Order of St. George 1st class for his illustrious accomplishment in saving Russia.

Thus, peace and order were once again restored, and Russia had risen from her death bed. While thebdevastation was considerable, and especially felt by the poor villagers, such wounds healed little by little while the losses were soon recouped through hard work and the help of the government.

So was destroyed the army of half a million men with which Napoleon feignedto conquer Russia. As if to ensure that no future European nation, even in alliance with others, would dare to attempt another invasion like this, fifty generals and 100,000 soldiers ended up as prisoners of war. In addition, we had 900 bronze guns, which Napoleon had abandoned during his flight from Moscow to Vilna, and with these our posterity would be able to build a magnificent monument to commemorate an event that is extraordinary in the annals of world history and serves as a testament to the glory of the great and powerful Russian empire.

On 12 [24] December, our artillery departed from Paradomino toward Grodno, where we were assigned our winter quarters. The following day we arrived at Oishishki, where we heard stories from local Jews about the treachery of the Lithuanian inhabitants, who, in the earlier stages of the campaign, had often attacked supply trains that were left poorly protected, slaughtered the sick and even captured a squad of jagers and their officer in Oishishki itself. Local landlords and gentry were especially influenced by the proclamations coming from the Duchy of Warsaw; they considered Napoleon as a restorer of ancient Poland. The remarkable exploits of Napoleon, who made all of Europe, except for Russian and Britain, tremble, his enterprising spirit and, finally, his incredible luck made everything seem possible. As life shows, all great enterprises seem ridiculous and absurd only after they turn out to be unsuccessful, while even the most reckless and audacious deeds, if successful, are glorified as the results of genius and the men who attempted them called great.

During our marches we occasionally had to stop at the *folwarks* of local landlords. They received us as if they were guilty, consumed with fear and apprehension at the animosity they expected from us. But, as a noble warrior acts with enmity only in battle, we soon disabused them of their worries, and through our mild and peaceful conduct we put them at their ease. Beautiful Polish women greeted us cautiously but they could easily disarm even the most hostile Muscovite with their charming smiles and delightful eyes. These *curecki*[6] expressed their sorrow that the war had required such great sacrifices and caused such extreme devastation to local inhabitants, saying that they never wanted the restoration of their homeland, but just for Poland to remain in peace and well provided for. Such eloquence, coming from such pretty lips, bewitched us and we of course believed them. [Yet] almost every house here had portraits of Napoleon. On such occasions, the *pani* [mistress of the house], noticing our interest in the portrait, usually told us that *the great Napoleon* [author's emphasis] had referred to himself as a "*niezgrabny* [unshapely] Frenchman" but "there, look at his head, a wellspring of goodness [*mostse dobrodzeyu*]," she would add in a particular tone, shaking her head, and letting us surmise the rest.

As language and faith represent the main differences between people who cannot find affinity and continue to sustain mutual hatred and want of understanding, the Poles must, out of necessity, join the Russians in one great tribe of Slavic people, to form one powerful

---

6 From Polish córka, meaning daughters.

state [*derzhava*] with one common law and faith. The Polish language differs only slightly from the Russian, and both languages share the same root. In a sincere brotherly union, the Polish language could easily form a dialect; the Polish faith is the same [as the Russian] - Christian, though with certain differences when it comes to rites. What is needed then is love that would make these brethren people cast aside their mutual hatred. If the matter is considered impartially, it becomes obvious that the Poles will only be happy when they extinguish in their hearts the flames of animosity that they feel toward Russians, their innocuous brethren, and join them to form a fraternal union within a joint powerful state. Due to its geographic location in Europe, Poland can never exist separate from Russia, for it could never become so powerful as to avoid the influence of this great empire; therefore, it must come to terms with reality and substitute its agreeable dream of national freedom for a stark reality of indispensable dependence, and enjoy the peace and tranquility that Russia can bestow on Poland under the protection of her mighty wing.[7]

On 18 [30] December, we arrived at Grodno. The last march proved to be unbearable as we suffered from wind and rain that blinded us. At least the Russian winter had relented, having made its contribution to the destruction of the foreign enemy.

Grodno proved to be quite a large town that had good-looking stone buildings, which, however, are begrimed [*zakoptelyi*] and in disrepair on account of their antiquity. Along with many private properties, of which the best were the old *oberża* [tavern] and the house where General Miloradovich stayed, the main square featured

---

7 Radozhitskii was an avid supporter of the Russian empire-building and an early proponent of pan-Slavism, the latter-day influential movement that emphasized a common ethnic background among the various Slavic peoples of eastern Europe. Like many Russian pan-Slavists, Radozhitskii argued that it was Russia's historic mission to unite the Slavic peoples into a Russian-dominated confederation and gain political dominance in eastern Europe.

the gorgeous cathedral of Saint Francis.⁸ The burgers, the *szlachta* [gentry] and anyone who was French had fled to Warsaw upon the approach of the Russians, so many houses were empty. The town had been occupied by the partisan, Davydov, seven days prior to our arrival. Instead of townsfolk, we mostly encountered soldiers and Austrians or Hungarians who had been released from the hospital. The enemy had abandoned numerous sick soldiers in the town, but at least there were no corpses in the streets, nor any charred ruins of houses and any of those signs of calamities that we had witnessed before. Along with its stables, the old palace⁹ was converted into a hospital that accommodated several thousand sick and wounded Austrians and French. A Russian church had been turned into a fodder store, and the meek faces of saints, with their eyes so full of blessings, could be seen peeping from behind mounds of oats and bundles of hay. Upon seeing this, our soldiers were disgusted and remarked that the saints had justly punished the unbelievers. At one supply depot, in particular, the French had abandoned several thousand rations of white biscuit that were given to our soldiers. These biscuits, looking like white bricks, were unleavened and the Russians did not like them, preferring their own biscuit, black and sour though it was.

To our delight, there were several *oberżas* [taverns] where, after months of surviving on dry biscuit and for just a small fee, we could finally pamper our taste buds with delicious Polish dishes and treat ourselves to coffee (as is well known, nowhere in Europe is coffee as well-prepared as in Poland). As it is customary in all Polish cities, the local taverns featured lovely women who attracted our men with what they had to offer: they were to be found at the heart of any group of officers making merry, and their cordiality was such that

---

8 The Cathedral of St. Francis Xavier, a splendid example of high Baroque architecture, was constructed between 1678 and 1652.

9 The Old Grodno Castle, first built in stone by Grand Duke Vytautas and thoroughly rebuilt in the Renaissance style by Scotto from Parma at the behest of Stefan Batory, one of the greatest Polish kings who died here in December 1586.

they often made us forget about undercooked or overly salted dishes of unskilled local cooks.

The fair sex in Poland is so distinctive that, even among the women of the lower classes, there are many who are very pretty, and plenty of Russian officers could boast of the special affection that these beauties showed them. But who was the happiest to see the Russians return? It was, of course, the Jews. Indeed, what is there for them not to like in living with the Muscovites [*Moskolyami*]? Our officers generously rewarded them for their services [*faktorstvo*]... while the Jews bought diverse items from our soldiers at a great profit. Despite the wartime conditions, their shops were open in every town, while their women, sitting around stoves like the ancient Pythias,[10] traded in all sorts of things.

We took the best quarters in town, not because of local hospitality, but rather because most of the houses were empty and only Jews and minor gentry remained in town. All the enthusiastic [Polish] patriots, fearing Russian vengeance, fled with their imaginary [French] saviors until the gracious [Russian emperor's] manifesto of 12 [24] December assuaged them of their unsubstantiated fears and persuaded them return to their homes and acknowledge the generosity of the mighty sovereign of Russia.

Thus ended the famous Russian War [*voina Rossiiskaya*]! Preparations for it were vast, the fighting was terrible, and its consequences – profound. Like a dreadful hurricane whose mighty wind devastates everything on its path or like a blazing lava that consumes everything on its course, Napoleon marched with his mighty host for one thousand *verstas* from the Nieman to Moscow

---

10 The Pythia was the legendary priestess who pronounced the words of spoken by the famous oracle at the temple Temple of Apollo at Delphi, located on the slopes of Mount Parnassus in Greece. As Radozhitskii uses it, the reference is anything put complementary: the very name derives from the smell of rottenness associated with the shrine - a consequence, this, of the sulferous hallucinogenic vapours that have been offered as one explanation of the weird and wonderful sayings that emanated from the oracle - while the Phythia, sometimes referred to in western literature as the Pythoness, was invariably described as a hideous crone.

and back, unleashing all the horrors of a disastrous war and producing calamities that eventually destroyed the great forces of France and the rest of Europe. This war marked the first step towards the crushing of Napoleon's colossal power. In six months, his vast plans that threatened to overthrow the Russian Monarchy, unchallengeable as it was for six centuries, had been all thoroughly defeated and only wreckages of lost battles, burning settlements, and dead corpses denoted the path that this genius, this destroyer of mankind, had followed.

Two powers [Russia and Britain] could still challenge the power of Napoleon, but he could confront only one of them. And strike he did at Russia, like a stormy sea breaking on a granite rock, whose lofty tip, firm in its foundations, scorned all the efforts of the violent tempest. If Europe no longer groans under the heavy yoke of its mighty conquerors and instead enjoys the old order of things, she owes all of it, of course, to Russia: the fire of Moscow, this unprecedented sacrifice of the love of the Fatherland, shone like the beacon of salvation for the whimpering prisoner that Europe then was. The giant was thoroughly dazed and with hundreds of thousands of soulless bodies scattered along his path, he had become weak. In vain were Napoleon's subsequent efforts to miraculously sprout new armies. He could no longer marshal warriors forged in the kilns of victories, only meager younglings who felt exhausted under the weight of their weapons.

The European powers, confronted by the feebleness of the conqueror who had hitherto trampled all over their rights but who was now disarmed by Russia, at last came to their senses. They grasped that the time has come to throw off the burdensome yoke and seek national independence with the help of the Russian arms. And so they came under Russian auspices: the formidable appearance and the vast size of forces that Russia wielded had dragged these powers into an alliance with her. Having defeated the enemy who had encroached on her own freedom, Russia now embarked on breaking the shackles of slavery that Napoleon had imposed on Europe.

END OF VOLUME 1

Index

A

adjutant, 22, 26–28, 46, 87, 110, 144
Alba (Prince Radziwill's estate), 12
alcohol, 8, 48
Aleksandrovo, 108
ambushes, 68, 112, 109, 119, 123, 125
Antichrist, 1, 4–5, 62, 98–99
Antonov fire (gangrene), 49
Apocalypse, 93
Aristovo, 130
artillery, viii–ix, 8–9, 11–12, 14, 17–22, 24–25, 32, 34–36, 39–43, 47, 52–53, 61–63, 65–66, 69–72, 76, 78, 81–89, 99–102, 107, 109–110, 112, 117–119, 126–128, 142, 144–145, 149–150, 152, 155–156, 162–163, 165, 167–169
Attila the Hun, 6
Augereau, Jean, 155
Austerlitz, 90

Austria, 2
Austrians, 81, 172

B

Babel, tower of, 107
Babenkovo, 108
Babinovichi, 38
Badenese, 81
Baggehufwudt/Baggovut, Karl Gustav von, 128
Bagration, Peter, 8, 30, 50, 54–55, 59
Bakhmetyev, general. 40
Barclay de Tolly, Michael, 11, 22, 30, 47, 50, 57, 61, 63, 67, 71, 98, 103
Bashkirs, 109
Batory, Stefan, 172
Bautzen, vii
Bavarian/Bavarians, 81, 107, 164
bayonets, 1, 65, 67-68, 81, 83–85, 136, 138, 143–146
bearskin, 53, 92, 167
Beelzebub, 4
Bennigsen, Levin von, 126, 128

Benyakony, 11
Berezina, 162, 164–165
Berlin, 17
Berthier, Alexander 68
Bistrom, Adam von 19–20, 22
Bobruisk, 12–13
Bogdanovo, 168
books, iv, 93, 54, 119, 143
boots, 46–47, 66, 113, 151, 155, 166
Borodino, v, vii, 57, 76–77, 79–81, 84–87, 89–90, 92, 94–95, 105, 107, 113, 141
Borovsk, 105, 130–131, 133–135
bridge, 19, 21–22, 27, 29, 34, 61–63, 72,98, 100–101, 111, 126, 164–165
Bronikowski, Nicolas, 164
Bykhov, 50

C

caissons, 35, 43–44, 61, 65, 87, 121, 130, 135, 141, 149–150, 168
cakes, 107
calamities, 98, 148, 155, 166–167, 172, 174
camp/campsites, 4, 17–18, 25-26, 28–34, 36, 39, 46, 54–55, 57–59, 70, 72, 75, 78, 91, 93–94, 97, 106, 109, 113–115, 119–120, 123, 125–126, 129–131, 135, 138, 141-142, 148-149, 151–152
canister, 20, 42–43, 45–47, 65, 71, 87, 117, 127, 142–144
cannon, 3, 10, 19–21, 35, 39, 41–46, 63–68, 71, 82–87, 91, 100, 102, 107, 112, 121, 127, 137, 143, 145, 149, 152, 160, 163, 165, 167-168
Caulaincourt, Auguste-Jean-Gabriel de, 85
cavalry, 22, 29, 31, 38, 42–43, 45–48, 50, 58, 63, 65–66, 71–72, 78, 84–86, 91, 105–108, 110, 112, 122–123, 126, 128–129, 133–135, 141–142, 145, 149, 152, 156.
cemetery, 149–150, 153
centaurs, 111
Cherneshnya, 126, 130
Chervonnaya, 156
Chichagov, Admiral Pavel, 105, 164–165, 168
Choglokov, Pavel, 14, 40, 42, 84, 141–142, 145–146
Chorąży, 11
church, 54, 72, 93, 95, 98, 102, 124, 135–137, 172
civilian, 35, 51, 99, 148
clergy, 115
Corsican, 1–2
Cossacks, 17, 19–21, 23, 25–26, 29, 31–32, 51–52, 54, 60,

INDEX

65–66, 70–71, 79, 84, 88, 91–92, 106-107, 121-122, 124, 126, 128, 130, 132, 135, 137–139, 141–146, 155–156
Courland, 3, 55
Crimea, 118
Croats, 81
cuirassiers, 83, 85, 124, 126, 129–130, 140, 155

D

Danes, 81
Daugėliškis, 22
Davout, Louis-Nicolas 30, 61, 134–135, 144, 156
Davydov, Denis, vii, 115, 172
Dnieper, 50, 53–54, 56, 59–63, 69, 72, 103, 162, 164
Dokhturov, Dmitry, 23, 25–26, 60, 62–63, 126, 130–133
Doomsday, 5, 98
Dorogobuzh, 60, 70–72, 145, 149, 151–152, 159
Dorokhov, Ivan, 14, 107, 124–125, 130–132, 137
dragoons, 26, 39–40, 78, 87, 107, 109–111, 144, 155
Dukhovshchina, 53, 159
Durrenstein, 74
Durykino, 75
Dvina, v, 15, 29–30, 32–36, 38, 50, 55

E

Essen, Magnus Gustav von, 3

F

Fabius (Quintus Fabius Maximus Verrucosus Cunctator), 105
Figner, Alexander, 13, 20, 52, 58–59, 65–66, 68, 76, 78, 82–84, 87–89, 94–95, 97, 99–102, 115, 117–124, 130, 142, 144, 149–150, 155–156, 163
fortifications, 13, 23, 29, 33, 60
fortress, 13, 60, 117
France, vii–viii, 2, 5, 114, 155, 174

G

Gaidukovshizna, 27
gangrene, 49
German/Germans, viii, 1, 24, 30-32, 37, 79, 117–119, 153–154
Germany, 2, 117, 160
ghosts, 4, 36, 53, 153, 158
ghouls, 132
Golovino, 138
Goncharovo, 134
Gorbunovo, 64
Gorki, 83–87
Grabbe, Pavel, 122
grenades, 42, 61

grenadiers, 65, 67–68, 83-84
Grodno, v, 55, 162, 169, 171–172
Gudin, Charles Etienne, 67
guerrillas, 120, 155
gunpowder, 42, 86, 101, 150
Gzhatsk, 75, 115, 138, 141

H
headquarters, 7, 13, 21, 36, 69, 97, 102, 108, 121, 125
Hebrew, 4
Hungarians, 172
hussars, 27-28, 38-39, 42–43, 51, 53, 66, 71, 84, 107, 115, 122, 142, 150
hyenas, 53

I
Icon, 62, 95, 124, 136
Italian/Italians, 32, 53, 79, 81, 107, 117–118, 121, 132-133, 156, 168

J
jagers, 19-21, 39, 40, 43, 51, 66–67, 69, 77, 84, 110, 126-127, 129, 142–144, 169
Jews, 7, 36–37, 162–163, 169, 173
Junot, Andoche 65

K
Kaidanov, 164
Kaluga, 4, 106, 108–109, 111, 130, 132–134

Kamenski, Nikolai 118
Kolocha, river 76–78, 84
Kolotsk, 77
Konovnitsyn, Dmitri 48, 60, 62–63, 68, 77
Kopunje, 19
Kopys, 162–164
Korff, Fedor 22, 24–25, 63–64, 67, 141
Kotlyarov, colonel A. 8, 11, 13, 52, 58
Krasnyi, v, vii, 59, 61, 149, 156, 160–162
Kremlin, 98, 102, 120
Kuplya, 112
Kutaisov, Alexander 12, 67, 83
Kutuzov, Mikhail (Golenischev-Kutuzov) 73–75, 77–79, 83, 86, 90–91, 95–97, 100, 106, 114, 120, 122, 125–126, 130, 134, 159–160, 162, 168–169

L
lancers, 26, 31, 38, 45–47, 83, 143–144
Letashevka, 126
Lithuania, 11, 13–14
Lubino, vii, 64–65, 68–69
Lyakhov, 155

M
Maloyaroslavets, v, 19, 113, 131–135, 137
Maslovo, 77

INDEX

Miloradovich, Mikhail, 75, 83, 87, 89, 91–92, 97, 109–112, 129, 131, 134, 137–138, 141, 144–145, 152, 155, 162, 171
Mir, 31
Mogilev, 50, 55
Moldavia, 95, 117-118
Moscow, v, vii, ix, 4, 17, 62, 64, 69–70, 76–77, 79, 81, 88, 91, 93–108, 111, 114–116, 119–120, 122, 124–125, 129, 135, 139, 146, 148, 157, 160, 162, 167, 169, 173–174
Mozhaisk, 76–77, 86, 89, 91, 106–107, 115, 121–122, 133–134, 138, 141, 157
Murat, Joachim 83, 95, 129–130
Music/musicians, 12, 18, 33, 63, 75, 104, 126

N

Naples, 74, 82, 110
Napoleon, vi–ix, 1–7, 11, 15–17, 29–31, 34–35, 47, 49–51, 53, 55–56, 59–63, 68–70, 74–75, 77–79, 81, 85–87, 90–95, 103–107, 114–116, 120, 122, 124–126, 130–135, 145, 147, 151, 153–154, 157, 160, 164–166, 169–170, 173–174
Nara, river 92, 126
Nesvizh, 3–8, 12, 46–47, 164

Neverovskii, Dmitri, 59–60
Nieman, river 9, 14, 35, 164, 173
nymphs, 36

O

opolchenye, 76–77, 79, 88, 91, 114
Orany, 14
Orlov-Denisov, Vasily, 67, 126, 128
Ornano, Philippe Antoine, 43
Orsha, 124
Oshmyany, 168
Osterman-Tolstoy, Alexander, 24 25, 28, 39, 43, 47, 67, 108, 109–111, 156, 162
Ostrovno, vii, 38, 52
Oudinot, Nicolas, 125, 164

P

Pakhra, 4, 101–102, 106, 108
Panki, 99
Parnassus, 173
Paskevich, Ivan, 109–111, 144–145
peasants, 24, 51, 59, 76, 113, 115, 119–121, 123, 125, 138–141, 157-158, 164
Platov, Matvei, 31, 54, 57, 71, 91, 114, 145, 159
plunder/plundering, 10, 52, 72, 79, 104, 107-108, 119, 124, 136, 155, 162

, 170–173
, 2, 5-7, 9, 12-13,
.-25, 31, 35, 46, 60, 79,
., 93, 107, 115, 118, 121,
129, 136, 164, 167, 169-173
Polotsk, 34–35, 125, 164
Poltava, 29–30, 103–104
Poniatowski, Józef Antoni,
109–110, 129
Portuguese, 81
Prudische, 63
Prussians, 17, 81
Pskov, 59, 117–118

R
Rayevskii, Nikolai, 60
rearguard, 19–23, 27, 32, 51, 64,
70–73, 77, 91–92, 97, 107,
109–112
Rostopchin, Fedor, 111
Rudnya, 57
Ryazan, 99–100

S
saber, 39, 43, 45, 66, 68, 85, 136
Saxons, 81
Schlippenbach, 43, 46, 52, 122
Scythians, 55
Sebezh, 125
Serfs/serfdom, 24, 125
servant, 10, 47, 99
Seslavin, Alexander, 115, 124,
130, 150, 168

Shuvalov, Pavel, 9, 12, 17,
24, 82
Slonim, 8, 12
Smolensk, v, vii, 34, 50, 52–55,
57, 59–64, 69–70, 73, 76–77,
86, 103, 105, 108, 130, 133,
150, 156–157, 160, 169
Spain, 81
Spaniards, 79, 81, 107
Sparta, 16
Steinheil, Faddei, 164
Suvorov, Alexander, 1, 16, 31,
74–75, 112, 145, 159

T
Tarutino, v, 93, 96, 111, 113,
115, 119–120, 125–126,
129–131, 142, 151–152
tavern, 7–8, 15, 17, 36, 38–39,
166, 171-172
tea, 12, 33, 37, 130, 146, 154,
157, 163
Thermopylae, 16
tobacco, 4–5, 8, 37, 44, 58
Tolstoy, Leo, ix
Tormasov, Alexander, 105, 165
Tuchkov (Tuchkov I), Nikolai,
17, 77
Tuchkov (Tuchkov III), Pavel
64–65, 68
Tula, viii, 104, 106, 108
Turks, 31, 117
Tutolmin, adjutant, 46–51

INDEX

U
uhlans, 84, 91, 122, 129
Ukraine, 7, 35
Uvarov, Fedor, 58, 84, 145
Uxkull, Boris von, vii

V
Valuevo, 77
Valutina Gora, vii, 68
Vereya, 105–106, 125, 133–134
Vilna, v, 9–11, 15, 17–19, 37, 55, 101, 118, 165–166, 168–169
Vinkovo, 130
Vistula, 168
Vitebsk, 34, 38–39, 55, 63, 73
Vladimir, vii–viii, 106
Volhynia, 35
Volkovysk, 9
Voronovo, 109–111
Vyazma, v, vii, 72, 74, 115, 132–134, 142–143, 149–152, 157

W
wagons/transports, 46, 54, 89, 99, 121, 129–130, 143, 150, 165
Warsaw, 2, 4, 170, 172

Westphalians, 81, 107
Wilkomir, 168
Wilson, Robert, 64, 67
Wittgenstein, Peter, 34, 125, 164, 168
women, 4, 24–25, 37–38, 62, 98, 113, 129, 138–140, 146–147, 162, 165–166, 170, 172–173
wounded, vii, 23, 39–40, 45–48, 51, 53, 71, 83–84, 88–89, 92, 124, 129, 137, 144–146, 153–154, 165, 172

Y
Yaroslavl, 54, 106
Yelnya, 133–134
Yermolov, Alexei, vii, 97, 100, 163

Z
Zaimishche, 72, 141
Zelva, 9
Zemlino, 91